The Employability Journal

Barbara Bassot

 macmillan education   palgrave

First published 2017 by
PALGRAVE

Palgrave in the UK is an imprint of Macmillan Publishers Limited, registered in England, company number 785998, of 4 Crinan Street, London, N1 9XW.

Palgrave® and Macmillan® are registered trademarks in the United States, the United Kingdom, Europe and other countries.

ISBN: 978–1–137–60381–4   paperback

This book is printed on paper suitable for recycling and made from fully managed and sustained forest sources. Logging, pulping and manufacturing processes are expected to conform to the environmental regulations of the country of origin.

A catalogue record for this book is available from the British Library.

A catalog record for this book is available from the Library of Congress.

Printed in China

Contents

List of Figures

Acknowledgements

I would like to express my sincere thanks to my family and friends for their tireless support in the process of bringing *The Employability Journal* to fruition. In particular I would like to thank Martin Bassot for his careful work on the diagrams and Marc Bassot for his proofreading and constructive comments. I would like to thank all the students who gave me permission to include their quotes, which are included in boxes in the text. These have inspired me and I am sure will inspire others. I would also like to thank my clients who I have worked with, whose stories and experiences have enabled me to write this book; some of them have become case studies or aspects of them. I would also like to thank my Commissioning Editor, Helen Caunce, for her belief in the project, and to the publisher for being prepared to take a risk with another new type of publication.

The author and publishers would like to thank the following publishers and organisations for permission to reproduce copyright material: Taylor and Francis for Figure 2 on page 7 from B. Bassot, *The Reflective Practice Guide* (2016); Wiley for Figure 3 on page 9 from C.L. Cooper, *Theories of Group Processes* (1976); The Career Development Institute for Figure 1 on page x.

Introduction

Welcome to *The Employability Journal*. Whatever your current programme of study, you will be concerned about what your future has in store for you when you graduate. In the past it is fair to say that a degree could be seen as a passport to a good job. When the number of people graduating from universities was smaller, simply having a degree could single you out in the eyes of an employer. Equally, graduates could expect a job at a certain level with a good salary, a so-called 'graduate job'. With increasing numbers of people gaining university degrees, this is no longer the case and it is now widely recognised that graduates need more than just their degree; they also need some form of work experience. This can be summed up in a phrase that you have probably heard already: 'a degree is not enough'.

However, getting experience is not the only important thing as, sadly, not all experience is good experience. In addition, it is very easy to go into a placement or an internship and to be very unclear about what you want to gain from it, missing learning opportunities and failing to understand how you can use the whole experience to inform your career decisions. This book is written for all university students and is designed to help you to reflect on your experience and thereby to enhance your career and professional development.

The whole concept of career can be very difficult to grasp.

The Career Learning and Development Bridge

In my own work (Bassot, 2009; Barnes, Bassot and Chant, 2011; Bassot, Barnes and Chant, 2014) I have developed the model of the Career Learning and Development (CLD) Bridge as a way of explaining the abstract concept of career, and career development in more detail (see Figure 1). The CLD Bridge is a suspension bridge; these bridges gain their strength from the tension in the cables and compression in the towers. These work together to carry the weight of the road, and keep everything in balance; without this balance, the bridge would collapse. I chose the metaphor of a suspension bridge because it clearly illustrates the tensions that many people experience between what they want as individuals and what is available to them in their context. The metaphor of the suspension bridge harnesses these tensions, and indeed relies on them in order to function effectively. This shows that in relation to career, these tensions can be seen as opportunities for growth rather than threats, but without denying the many challenges that they bring.

Because of constant and rapid changes in the labour market, the CLD Bridge operates with two-way traffic. This reminds us of the need to engage in continuous professional development (CPD), in order to develop ourselves and to meet the needs of our employers. Career then is something that we construct throughout our lives and not a 'one-off' decision. To many this will be a relief, as the idea of a decision I make (or a mistake I have to live with) for the rest of my life becomes less and less the norm.

Figure 1 shows three aspects of the CLD Bridge. First, on the left-hand side is career happiness; this is focused on you as an individual. Second, on the right-hand side is career resilience. This means being able to 'bounce back' from disappointments and being positive about challenges that the labour market presents. The road spanning the Bridge represents career growth (Bassot, Barnes and Chant, 2014) and is based on Vygotsky's (1978) concept of the zone of proximal development (ZPD). The focus of learning

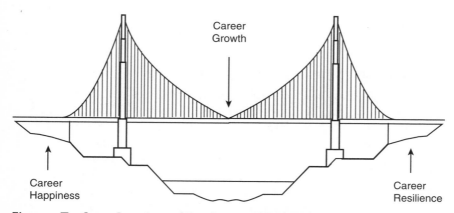

Figure 1 The Career Learning and Development (CLD) Bridge

and development in the ZPD is on my next steps rather than what is far ahead in the distance. I can make progress within the ZPD by gaining useful practical experience and by having discussions with others who are more knowledgeable than I am (for example my mentor and experienced colleagues), which enables career growth.

I will refer to aspects of the CLD Bridge where appropriate throughout *The Employability Journal*. This book can be used in a number of ways to enhance your career learning and development. Unlike most other academic books, this is a book that you write in – and I encourage you to do so! It is something that you can put into a bag or backpack to use whenever you need it, for example while you are travelling to work, on placement or volunteering. You can work through it from start to finish, or select those topics that are the most relevant and interesting at a particular time. It is a tool to help you to reflect on your experiences, enabling you to take a deeper approach to your learning and career development by understanding more about yourself and your future.

So why should you write in this book? As a cognitive process, writing helps us to develop our understanding because it involves processing our thoughts. Neuroscience shows us that writing stimulates the reticular activating system at the base of the brain, which enables us to concentrate and focus our attention. In short, it is very difficult to write something by hand whilst doing something else and, as a result, we are much more likely to remember something we have written down. In addition, a written record is something we can go back to later. Many of us assume that we will remember things, especially when we feel they are significant at the time. But in reality, we can even forget things that we were sure we would remember at the time, particularly when our daily lives are busy. This can also happen during those times when lots of things are new to us, for example whilst on placement.

Bearing in mind that a degree no longer guarantees anyone a job, making yourself as employable as possible is important. This involves presenting yourself in the best possible light to people who might become your future employers. However, before you can do that, you need to be as clear as you can about the kind of work you would like to do after graduation; reaching this point can in itself be a difficult and daunting task for a number of reasons. Here are some of them and you may be able to think of more.

1   It is very difficult to be sure that you want to do something in the future without having an opportunity to try it for yourself. Speaking to people about what they do will certainly help, but only to an extent. In order to explore your options, you need opportunities to at least try some of them out. Here work experience, placements and volunteering come into their own. However, it is not always a good idea to try lots of different things one after another as this can be confusing. A good strategy is to think through your strengths, skills and values, as these will help you to assess your interests, which in turn will guide you towards things that you will enjoy and at the same time will help you to avoid unnecessary disappointments.

2   There is a much wider variety of career opportunities available now than in the past. The more options you have the more difficult it becomes when making choices, and for this reason it is simply more difficult for many people to make career decisions now than it used to be.

3   Making important decisions is often difficult because of the fear of making mistakes. This is particularly the case when it comes to making career decisions. For this reason many people put off making these kinds of decision for fear of choosing 'the wrong thing'. Ultimately this can result in drifting into something when time runs out, which for some can work out fine, but for others can again be a mistake.

4   The labour market is constantly changing, and because of the peaks and troughs in the economy many people today do not make a career decision for life; rather, they make a decision about their next step. This is actually very helpful in relation to the previous point as this can greatly reduce the 'fear factor'. However, it also means that a lot of flexibility and resilience is required in order to 'take the rough with the smooth'.

5   The labour market itself is now much more flexible than it used to be; this means that there are fewer clear pathways to follow and many different ways of reaching the same destination. For example, in the past, if you did not start to train as a plumber or electrician when you were 16 as an apprentice, it simply would not be possible to do this later. Today this is

far from the case and whilst changing your career direction is now easier, there are many more training routes to choose from, which again makes things much more complicated.

6   It is well known that many job vacancies are never advertised. This means that networking with people and trying to put yourself in the right place at the right time can be of paramount importance. For some people this comes easily, but for others it doesn't.

In short, making yourself as employable as possible will be an ongoing process.

Employability is defined as

> a set of achievements – skills, understandings and personal attributes – that make graduates more likely to gain employment and be successful in their chosen occupations, which benefits themselves, the workforce, the community and the economy. (Yorke, 2006, p. 8)

From this definition, Dacre Pool and Sewell (2007) developed the CareerEDGE model that shows clearly what graduates need in order to put themselves in the strongest position to succeed in the labour market.

Career development learning – this involves helping students to acquire knowledge, concepts, skills and attitudes which will equip them to manage their careers, or their lifelong progression in learning and work. This can be done through sessions and modules, which could be optional or compulsory.

Experience (work and life) – opportunities to gain experience are vital in order to be clear about the future and to be able to compete in the labour market.

Degree subject knowledge, skills and understanding – these set graduates apart from those who have not studied at this level.

Generic skills – the skills needed in every area of work such as good time management and teamwork.

Emotional intelligence – being in tune with emotions is key to many aspects of working life, including being able to get on well with others and remaining motivated.

At the heart of the CareerEDGE model is reflection and evaluation, which helps to build the following three key aspects of personal development.

Self-efficacy – often referred to as self-efficacy beliefs. This is an individual's judgement of their ability to carry out actions in order to reach their goals. Those with a high level of self-efficacy believe that they are capable of organising themselves in order to achieve what they want to achieve.

Self-confidence – is a term used to describe an individual's trust in their own skills, abilities and aptitudes. Those with high self-confidence trust their own judgement.

Self-esteem – this term describes the value that the individual places on themselves and their feelings of personal worth. Those with high self-esteem value themselves and what they have to offer.

This book will help you to reflect on your learning from your experience and thereby help you to increase your self-efficacy, self-confidence and self-esteem; all of this will give you the potential to become more successful in the future. It is important to emphasise that this book is all about you and your future. In my experience, it is only when someone focuses on what they want to do, rather than on what others (for example friends and family) might want for them, that they feel fulfilled and satisfied at work. Most of us will spend more years at work than our parents and grandparents, so it is well worth investing some time to fathom out what you want to do in the future. In addition, most people spend most of their week at work, so it's important to enjoy it if you can.

As well as helping you to gain more understanding of yourself, *The Employability Journal* will also help you to understand more about some key aspects of working life which we often take for granted. For example, having some understanding of how teams work can help if you find yourself in a team that does not seem to be functioning well. In addition, it is important to be clear about how to behave in a work situation; today this is often much less about a rigid set of formalities and more about being aware of the culture of the organisation and how to fit in with the way things are done. Having some theoretical understanding of such issues will mean that you can learn more from your experiences.

How this book is organised

The Employability Journal is organised in three parts.

Part 1 is broken down into 12 themes. Each theme starts with a brief introduction and is followed by five pieces of content based on the theme where some key theories are introduced in an accessible way. These are followed by a number of blank pages for your written reflections, including some practical activities to help you to understand more about your experience by applying theory to it. Each theme also includes a case study to illustrate some of the points being made.

Part 2 contains further exercises along with more blank pages for reflective writing. These serve as further prompts for thinking critically about your career learning and development.

Part 3 focuses on CV building. This section contains pages to record significant activities – for example, meetings attended, presentations delivered, key achievements and key words to use at job interviews. It will serve as a helpful record for the future, particularly when you find yourself writing personal statements for job applications or programmes of postgraduate study.

Many people find that the time they spend writing reflectively is time invested. I hope that you find *The Employability Journal* helpful in your career learning and development.

Barbara Bassot

Part 1
Tools for reflection

Making the most of your experience

This section will help you to:

- ○ Think about what your placement can do for you and what you hope to gain from it
- ○ Understand the value of setting yourself some goals
- ○ Understand how we learn from experience
- ○ Identify who can help you get the experience you need
- ○ Understand the value in having a mentor and help you to find a good one.

What can your placement do for you?

Many employers today agree that qualifications alone are not enough; most look for experience too. So doing some kind of placement, part-time work or volunteering will add a lot to your CV, whilst boosting your confidence and your overall level of preparation for your future working life. In addition, it is very difficult to know if you will enjoy an area of work before you try it for yourself. Here are some of the things that you can gain from a placement.

○ Invaluable experience – if you already know what you would like to do when you graduate, gaining experience in this area can be very useful in helping to confirm this decision. It could even lead to an all-important job offer. Equally of course it could reveal that this area of work was not what you expected and can give you an opportunity to revisit your decision. If you are still unsure about what you want to do (and many undergraduates are – even some postgraduates too), a placement can offer you a good opportunity to try something you might be interested in.

○ Opportunities to explore what you would like to do in the future – even if you are clear about the kind of work you want, the same job, or one similar, can be very different depending on the sector or even the type of organisation in which it is offered. A placement can provide you with insights into the kind of employer you might like to work for in the future.

○ Personal insights – reading about different careers and what they entail is good, but direct experience ensures that your knowledge is accurate and current. It is also important to remember that the aim of written material (including things that are available online) will often be to 'sell' you a particular idea, depending on who it is written by.

○ Opportunities to begin to adjust to being at work – working life is often very busy and demanding and a placement will help you to experience this first-hand. It goes without saying that it will be very different from being at university and a placement will open your eyes to the demands ahead, which will help you to prioritise your job search.

○ Motivation for study – many students say that a placement motivates them in their studies as it gives them an idea of where they are heading and how they might use their degree. Some writers suggest that students who undertake placements gain better degree classifications whilst others say that high achieving students are the ones who tend to get good placements (Driffield et al., 2011); however, all agree that the quality of the placement is what counts.

○ Opportunities to learn more about yourself – in the area of career development we all need to continue to learn about ourselves. Jobs change and so do we; being aware of our strengths, likes and dislikes informs our decision making.

○ Opportunities to develop your skills – working life demands many skills, such as teamwork, interpersonal, negotiating and IT skills. A placement should give you the chance to develop in a number of different ways.

When thinking about where you might gain some useful experience, it is worth bearing in mind all of the points above.

Goals – 'Begin with the end in mind'

In many areas of life having clear goals helps us to achieve more. If we do not know what we want to achieve, we are unlikely to have a sense of direction and should not be surprised if after a while we feel that we are not making much progress. When thinking ahead, it is important to consider what we want to achieve; setting goals can be a very helpful way of articulating this.

Goals can be long term (for example, over a number of years but usually not more than five), medium term (for example, over the next six months or year) and short term (for example, over a week or a month). In order to set long-term goals, Covey (2004a) emphasises the importance of having a personal vision for the future. He urges us to 'Begin with the end in mind' (Habit 2 of *The 7 Habits of Highly Effective People*). Covey argues that our lives are created twice – first in our minds and then in practice. He argues that focusing on the end result or outcome is one way of helping us to begin to see things more clearly. Interestingly he also argues that if we do not have our own vision, we can live our life where the vision and priorities that others have for us are more important than our own.

Many agree that goals need to be SMART:

○ **S**pecific – goals that are too general will not give us a clear sense of direction or purpose, so goals need to contain a level of useful detail.
○ **M**easurable – we need to be able to measure our progress towards our goals and to know how we will be able to tell when we have achieved them.
○ **A**chievable – setting goals that we are unlikely to achieve is very dispiriting and can make us want to give up; however, goals also need to challenge us, as those that we can achieve too easily do not motivate us enough.
○ **R**ealistic – we need to be honest with ourselves about what we can do; we are unlikely to achieve goals that can only be reached in an ideal world.
○ **T**ime scaled – deadlines are important as they help us to keep on track and prevent us from wasting too much time through procrastination.

Goal setting can be a very positive process because when we achieve a goal it raises our motivation and encourages us to set more. This means we enter a cycle, often depicted as an upward moving spiral as in Figure 2.

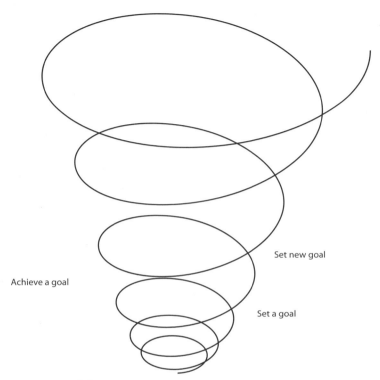

Achieve a goal

Set new goal

Set a goal

Figure 2 Goal theory

It is worth spending some time thinking about what you hope to achieve whilst on placement. Think about the following questions.

○ What are your long-term goals? Whether you have a specific career goal or not, imagine you are talking to a friend five years from now; how would you like to describe what you are doing?

○ What do you hope to achieve whilst on placement?

○ What are you looking forward to most?

○ What are the key areas that you feel you need to develop?

○ What could get in the way of your development?

○ How could you overcome the barriers to your development?

Try this

Make a list of five key areas that you would like to develop over the next few months. Now write some medium- and short-term goals to help you to make progress. These should help you to move towards your vision for your future or begin to formulate one.

'I have come to the realisation that I am more than capable of moving forward, and achieving a career goal I didn't realise I had.'

Learning from experience

Having thought about what your placement can do for you and what you hope to gain from it, it is also good to understand something of how we all learn from experience. In many different areas of work lots of learning happens on the job. Whilst it is good to read about certain careers and to talk to people who are involved in them, nothing can replace some first-hand experience in a work setting.

Kolb's (1984) experiential learning cycle offers insights into how we all learn from experience. There are four stages in the cycle which are depicted as following on from each other, as shown by the arrows in Figure 3.

In order to make the most of any experience, Kolb argues that we need to complete the cycle depicted in Figure 3. Following an experience, we need to reflect on it (Reflective Observation). Time spent reflecting is vital to

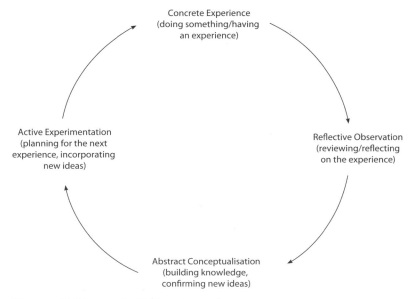

Figure 3 Kolb's experiential learning cycle
© 1975, by John Wiley & Sons, Ltd.

our progress; it is very easy in our busy lives to fail to do this and thereby to miss out on much of the learning that is taking place. As a result of our reflections we build our knowledge through Abstract Conceptualisation; in this case, knowledge is about ourselves (including our strengths, weaknesses, interests and dislikes) and of our possible future. This is followed by Active Experimentation, as our new knowledge enables us to think about how we might progress and do things next time. This includes considering alternative ways of doing things and additional experience that we might need to gain. All of this learning process may happen in a matter of moments, or over days, weeks or months, depending on the experience.

It is important to consider how you might be able to use the cycle in order to maximise the learning from your experience; here are some ideas.

○ Making time to reflect will be particularly important. It is all too easy to rush from one experience to the next without taking any time to think anything through. As a result your time in the workplace will soon be over and you will find it difficult to remember what you did and what you gained from it. This means that it could be difficult to discuss at a job interview, as you simply might not remember.

○ Consider using a tool for reflection. Many writers on the subject of reflective practice and experiential learning suggest keeping a reflective journal like this book to record your thoughts. This is very valuable on a number of levels, as discussed in the introduction to this book.

○ Practice using the cycle through discussion with someone else. This could be a fellow student, colleague, mentor or supervisor.

However, it is important to remember that any model that argues that things happen in a particular order always leaves itself open to critique – does it always happen like that? The answer is, probably not. So don't worry if you find yourself starting the cycle at different points depending on the circumstances. For example, a large-scale project will often begin with preparation, which could include identifying a number of different alternatives through Active Experimentation. In some circumstances research is needed first to build knowledge through Abstract Conceptualisation, and in the early days mistakes can be avoided through some Reflective Observation prior to jumping into an experience.

Try this   Think of an experience you have had recently and analyse it using Kolb's cycle. Was this helpful? If so, why? If not, why not?

'I have spent the majority of my time within the conceptualising stage of Kolb's model, trying to generate a hypothesis about what I have learnt.'

Theme 1.4 **Who can help you get the experience you need?**

Once you are clear about what you hope to gain from your experience in the workplace, it is then important to think about how you will best be able to get it; identifying key people in an organisation and building effective relationships with them will be vital to your development. In many situations (but not all) a short period of induction is organised to help you to become familiar with the organisation and its staff and this is an ideal time to begin to identify who you need to build links with in order to get the most from your experience. Here are some pointers:

○ Your manager or the person with overall responsibility for your time in the organisation – your relationship with this person will be a vital key to your success. If the work opportunity is well organised, you should meet this person soon after joining. Be sure to make a good first impression by being organised; remember the phrase, 'you only get one chance to make a first impression'. Having thought through what you hope to gain, and what your placement can do for you, be sure to take with you the goals you have set for yourself and discuss them. Most employers are happy if you take along ideas rather than leaving everything to them. Always remember that they are likely to be very busy people and it is good to show them that you have initiative – something that many employers value. Some well thought-out goals will help you and them to plan a very worthwhile placement.

○ Training and development – most large employers have a training and development department. Be sure to make contact with them to find out about opportunities for any relevant courses or seminars. You should keep a record of these (see Part 3) and include these in your CV.

○ Experienced colleagues in the department or section – being alongside experienced people to observe their work initially and then to get involved is an excellent way of learning. Be sure to show enthusiasm and to listen carefully to what they have to share and then offer to help with tasks that you feel you can do. Equally, try not to overcommit yourself or to volunteer to do something that you are not sure about. Not being able to 'deliver' could leave a negative impression; in the short term it is much better to ask for clarification first and to be open about what you think you can do, whilst also being receptive to doing more later, in relation to both the volume of work and its level of difficulty or complexity.

○ New employees and recent graduates – these people will be able to give you an insider's view on working for the organisation. Listening to their stories (for example, how they got their jobs, what they do in their day-to-day work, what they feel about the organisation) will be very helpful on a number of levels in relation to your decision making.

Finding a mentor

The *Cambridge English Dictionary* defines a mentor as 'a person who gives a younger or less experienced person help and advice over a period of time, especially at work'. So it is easy to see that having a mentor whilst on placement will be an excellent idea. In some situations, prior to joining an organisation, a mentor will already have been identified. In others, it might be something you need to suggest or even politely request. Either way, understanding something about the mentoring relationship will be very helpful. Here are some points to help you to find, and more importantly keep, a good mentor.

- Mentoring is like any other positive human relationship – your mentor needs to be someone you get on with and trust.

- Mentoring involves being open to feedback – mentoring without feedback may well not be very valuable (see Theme 6). However, all feedback needs to be constructive (pointing out the good things as well as the areas for development); being willing to listen, receive feedback and then act on it are all vital for a positive mentoring relationship. Remember that many mentors have been mentored themselves and will therefore expect constructive feedback from you too.

- Mentoring involves commitment on both sides – the vast majority of people at work are very busy, so taking on something that will be an extra time commitment for them will inevitably be challenging. Be sure to show your enthusiasm and commitment to the relationship as no one wants to mentor someone who is half-hearted about it. Otherwise they will probably simply say they don't have the time.

- Mentoring involves showing initiative – ideally mentoring is led by the mentee, so expect your mentor to ask you what you want to gain from it. This will help them to decide if they are the right person for this role and vice versa.

- Mentoring needs to be prioritised – in your initial meeting it is important to be clear about how often you would like to meet (not too often, but often enough to show that it is something you take seriously), for how long (usually no more than an hour) and the location (this does not always have to be on the employer's premises; offering to go to a local coffee shop can be useful as it can offer a more relaxed atmosphere and a degree of confidentiality). Once this has been established, be sure to keep to your side of the bargain.

○ Mentoring involves preparation – there is nothing more frustrating for a mentor than to make time to attend a mentoring session where the mentee has not thought about what they want to discuss. This often results in valuable time being wasted and understandably this makes mentors very unhappy! It is good to get into the habit of thinking about what you want to discuss with your mentor before the session and contacting them to let them know. This way you will both be well prepared and should have a useful session.

○ Mentoring involves appreciation – a good mentor welcomes being appreciated. Remember the phrase 'a little appreciation goes a long way' and be sure to show it!

Try this   Think about what you hope to gain from having a mentor. How can you show initiative to facilitate this? If you don't have a mentor, how might you be able to get one?

Case study: SMART goals

Theo is in the first year of a degree in French and Spanish and is keen to use his languages when he graduates. He has always enjoyed French, but is learning Spanish from scratch. He has secured a two-month summer job with an English language school in Spain. He hopes this will help him to improve his level of fluency in Spanish whilst beginning to explore how he could use his languages. As the time for starting his job approaches he becomes quite nervous of what lies ahead, particularly how he will cope with needing to speak Spanish regularly, which is still quite new to him. He knows that he will be working with other English-speaking students and wants to be sure not to spend the whole time teaching and speaking English. He decides to set some SMART goals to help him gain the most from his experience. Here are two examples.

Goal – develop my fluency in Spanish

Specific – speak Spanish with native speakers

Measurable – the number of people I speak to in Spanish each day

Achievable – learn 20 new Spanish words each week

Realistic – speak Spanish for no less than one hour per day

Time scaled – for the duration of the two months

Goal – begin to find out how I can use my French and Spanish when I graduate

Specific – speak to other students in the language school who are in their second and third years about their plans for the future

Measurable – the number of students in their second or third year spoken to

Achievable – speak to 10 students

Time scaled – during the two-month period

Theme 2

Self-awareness

This section will:

○ Introduce you to a strengths model

○ Engage you in self-analysis by using the SWOT and SWAIN approaches

○ Help you begin to explore your motivations and passions

○ Help you to identify some of your dislikes

○ Introduce you to the concept of learning styles.

A strengths-based approach

When thinking about the future it is vital to be clear about what you are good at and where your strengths lie. Most of us thrive in environments where we have the opportunity to be involved in activities where we can achieve, and that give us the chance to grow and develop. The workplace is no exception to this and before embarking on, for example, a placement or internship, it is important to think about the strengths that you will bring to it. This is also important because you are very likely to be asked about your strengths at an interview for a job or course of further study.

Strengths can be placed in the following categories:

- Skills – these are things that you can do well. Examples are communication (interpersonal, written, using digital media), IT, teamwork, technical, practical and organisational.
- Knowledge – this covers things that you know and understand. Examples are knowledge of processes, procedures, aspects of legislation, understanding of markets and consumer needs.
- Attitudes – these are sometimes referred to as personal qualities. Examples are motivation, enthusiasm, interest in fellow workers, commitment, having a strong work ethic, being conscientious, good timekeeping and showing appropriate initiative.

The fundamental idea behind the approach is that everyone has strengths and resources (such as family, friends, colleagues) that they can draw upon to maximise them. In short, we need to identify what we do well, do more of it and continue to develop it. In today's rapidly changing labour market no one can afford to sit back and assume that they have learned all there is to know in any particular area. A strength will soon become a weakness if we do not continue to learn and progress. Adopting a strengths-based approach will help you to grow in self-determination and build resilience (see Theme 3.4).

Try this   Now think about your strengths. Write some notes under the headings of knowledge, skills and attitudes.

Self-analysis – SWOT and SWAIN

Understanding your strengths is just one aspect of gaining self-awareness. In order to gain the most from any work experience, we need to know ourselves well. In this respect doing a SWOT analysis can be very helpful. SWOT stands for:

Strengths – things we do well. We looked at these in Theme 2.1.

Weaknesses – things we find difficult or could learn to do better. Like strengths, these are all very individual. What one person finds easy, someone else will find difficult; so we need to know what these are for ourselves not for others.

Opportunities – things that are available to us that could help us to improve. These could include such things as training, mentoring, coaching, networking and research.

Threats – things that could get in the way of our development. These can be practical, such as a lack of time or money, or deeper issues, such as a lack of confidence and fear.

In a SWAIN analysis, Opportunities and Threats are replaced by Aspirations, Interests and Needs.

Aspirations – these are things that we hope for in the future, including things we would like to achieve, goals we would like to reach (see Theme 1.2) and the kind of life we would like to lead. They can be specific and practical, such as a certain level of income, the chance to travel and see different parts of the world, or owning a particular model of car. They can also be more intangible, such as being respected and valued for what we do, making a valuable contribution to society or fulfilling our potential.

Interests – these are the things we enjoy doing and that we gain satisfaction from. Again, these are individual and vary from person to person.

Needs – in general the focus here is on the things we need to do in order to develop and achieve our potential. These can be specific, such as taking part in a particular aspect of training, or more general, such as growing in confidence.

Try this   Write in each of the boxes in Figure 4 to undertake your self-analysis.

Strengths

Weaknesses

Opportunities

Threats

Aspirations
Interests
Needs

Figure 4 SWOT/SWAIN analysis

Motivations and passions

Understanding your motivations and passions is another key aspect of gaining self-awareness. In order to make any kind of career decision you need to understand what motivates you and, perhaps more importantly, where your long-standing interests lie (see Theme 2.2). Passion might seem a strange word to use when thinking about career, but life is simply too short to be in a job you hate, only living for weekends and holidays, and dreading Sunday evenings – particularly when we bear in mind that we all have to work longer than our grandparents did! If you are still unsure about what your passions are, things that you have been interested in for a long time can give you some very important clues. Recognising your passions is a key step towards finding career happiness on the left-hand side of the CLD Bridge.

Here are some areas to think about to help you to identify what motivates you and where your passions lie.

When you were growing up, what did you love to do? Think about the things that you used to do when you were very young that you really enjoyed.

What do you love doing now? If you could choose to do anything in your spare time, what would it be?

What do you find really easy to do? Think about the things you do easily; remember that these are things that we often take for granted, and we can be prone to minimise them. So, if you find yourself thinking 'but anyone can do that' the answer probably is 'no, they can't!'

What do others see in you? Think about the times when other people come and ask you for help, support or assistance. These give indications of your skills and talents.

What gives you the energy to get out of bed in the morning? Think of those things that you really look forward to doing each day, week, month or year.

What do other people say about you? Listening to feedback from those around us is an important aspect of career development. Invariably people say things such as 'I think you'd be really good at ...' What feedback have you had? Of course it is important to remember that not all feedback is good feedback, and we might have reason to disagree with it (see Theme 6).

Try this   Under each heading, make a list of at least five things in response to the questions above and try to rank them in order of preference. Then look at everything you have written; are there any themes that stand out to you? If so, this could help you to identify your passions and to be clearer about what motivates you.

'A resilient, passionate and driven employee can learn new skills and is likely to make a greater contribution than someone with appropriate skills but no motivation and passion.'

Dislikes and assumptions

Understanding your dislikes and assumptions can also help you to become more self-aware. Some people who feel confused and uncertain about the future find it easier to talk about their dislikes than they do their interests. These are often things they know they do not want to do. Whilst this might appear negative on the surface, it can sometimes offer a helpful starting point. Every job, even one that we enjoy, has its downsides. When thinking about your time in the workplace, which aspects have you found least enjoyable?

Here are some questions that can help you to identify these:

What do you dislike about your current work experience? Think about particular tasks that you are asked to do that you do not enjoy. If you could choose to drop some of these, which would they be?

Which aspects of your current work experience do you find difficult? There are often (but not always) close links between what we find difficult and what we dislike. Think about the things you struggle with at work. What are they and why do you think this is?

What do you dread being asked to do by your manager or supervisor? Think about the past few weeks and identify tasks or projects that you wish you could have avoided. What might these be?

What is the least likeable part of your work? Think of those things that you really do not look forward to doing each day or week.

What do other people say about you? What do the people you work with say about the things you appear to dislike? If this is not apparent, try asking a trusted colleague for some feedback.

It is also very helpful to think about some of the assumptions you might be making about your future. Sometimes we are not aware of these until we deliberately spend a bit of time trying to explore them. Here are some more questions to help you to do this.

What do you assume you will be doing when you graduate? Think about the things you might already have said to people about this.

What do you assume you won't be doing? These might be prefaced in your mind by phrases such as 'I will never do a job where …' or 'I could never work for someone who …'

What do you assume will get in the way of your progress? This might be prompted by thoughts such as 'I could never do … because …'

Understanding more about what you dislike and the assumptions you might be making is helpful. Whilst you will not be able to avoid all of your dislikes when thinking about what you might do in the future, you can choose to focus on areas where their impact will be less; for example, they might give you clues about the kind of work to avoid. Many people can be limited by their assumptions, and whilst it is important to understand that it is not possible for a particular individual to do anything, most of us can do more than we think we can.

Learning styles

Understanding our learning styles is an important aspect of self-awareness; Honey and Mumford (2000) describe these as learning habits that we have acquired over the years. They can give us vital clues not only about why we act and react in certain ways, but can help us to understand our colleagues and managers better too. Understanding them will help us to gain more insights into our strengths and weaknesses.

Over a number of years Honey and Mumford (2000) carried out extensive work on the subject of learning styles and have identified the following four distinct styles. Each style has its relative strengths; however, in addition they each have allowable weaknesses which come to the fore when we overdo our strengths.

- **Activists** are doers who like to be involved in new experiences. They are open-minded and enthusiastic, enjoy getting on with things, and can achieve a lot in a short space of time. However, they can often go into a situation 'feet first' without enough forethought, so can be prone to making mistakes.

- **Reflectors** are thinkers who like to stand back and look at a situation from different perspectives. They enjoy collecting information and thinking about things carefully before reaching any conclusions. They like observing other people and listening to their views before offering their own. However, they can be seen as slow and might panic in a crisis when they don't have enough time to think.

- **Theorists** are analytical people who like to seek explanations for things. They often think problems through in a step-by-step way and can be perfectionists who like to fit things into a rational scheme or model. They have an ability to see things in a detached and objective way but at the same time can be seen as rather cold and calculating. However, they find things difficult when there are no rational explanations.

- **Pragmatists** are practical people who are keen to try out new ideas and prefer things that can be applied easily in practice. They enjoy problem solving and decision making but can become impatient when things do not appear to be working. They can also become cynical if they feel that an idea has been tried before and failed.

Most of us have a preference for more than one style. Strengths in all styles shows a strong, all-round learner – so in order to gain most from your experiences it is important to know your strengths and your least preferred styles; the latter will give you clear things to work on as you progress. Remember to look for the learning styles of others too, as this will help you to work well with your colleagues.

'My learning style is Activist; I tend to start my learning cycle by doing something. I often do not think things through beforehand, and if it goes wrong, I tend to try again without really considering what went wrong and why.'

Case study : Learning styles

Claudia really looked forward to her placement in the marketing department of a large company and was keen to show initiative. She has now been there for three weeks and has received some initial feedback on her performance. Several people in her team have commented positively on her enthusiasm and commitment but have also said that she seems to be rushing into situations and making silly mistakes. In preparation for a review meeting Claudia's manager summarises the feedback and asks her to complete the Learning Styles Questionnaire (Honey and Mumford, 2006).

Claudia completes the questionnaire before the meeting and realises for the first time that she has a very strong preference for the Activist style. Her score for the Reflector style is particularly low. She discusses her questionnaire results with her manager and realises that often her enthusiasm makes her act too quickly without taking time to think through the consequences. She realises that this is why she is making such mistakes.

During the meeting Claudia's manager asks her to think of some strategies to help her begin to overcome this. They agree together that she will

- Deliberately take a little time to think things through before acting
- Check with others if she is unsure of the consequences of her initial thoughts, rather than rushing in
- Explain the pitfalls that might occur as a result of her actions to an experienced colleague
- Write down what she feels she has learned from taking these steps for discussion at her next review meeting.

Claudia soon realises the benefits of taking a bit more time to think before acting. Her colleagues notice too and make positive comments about her progress.

Theme 3

Career development

This section will:

- ○ Help you to build your understanding of the term career and what it means today
- ○ Help you to understand the importance of being strategic when making career decisions
- ○ Focus on how you can find career happiness
- ○ Enable you to learn how to build career resilience
- ○ Help you to consider your next steps to achieve career growth.

What does the term career mean today?

The word career is used regularly in everyday conversation and is probably a term that most people think they understand. For most people the words work and career are synonymous, and in particular for many it will mean some kind of paid work. For some students the word career can be difficult as it feels as though it can pose the question 'what am I going to do with the rest of my life?' Making career decisions can be daunting and even scary as 'the stakes are high'.

In the past the word career often meant 'what I'm going to do when I leave school or graduate.' It implied some kind of paid work that you stayed in for a considerable length of time, perhaps even for the duration of your working life. People often started on relatively low pay with some form of apprenticeship or training, followed by structured progression up a kind of ladder.

During the late 1970s and 1980s the structure of the UK labour market began to change, as many manufacturing industries struggled to compete in global markets. Over a number of years, the UK economy moved from one based on manufacturing industries to one based on the service sector. During this period many more people began to study at university; in the global marketplace there was a recognition that highly skilled and innovative people were needed to enable the UK as a nation to compete on an equal footing. However, as the number of graduates increased, so did the competition for jobs following graduation.

Like any other area of life, in a world of rapid change the future of career is difficult to predict. Some writers (Edwards, 1993; Storey, 2000) have suggested that change is so prevalent and rapid that the whole idea of a career with progression up a ladder is outdated. Many argue that all workers need to be flexible, transferring their skills and knowledge from one contract to the next as new business is generated in response to changes in consumer demand. Career becomes a more general term, meaning a pathway through life and people can expect to work in several different job roles during a lifetime. Others, however, state that such claims are exaggerated (Noon and Blyton, 2007). In general, though, the future remains uncertain when the only constant seems to be change.

Try this   Have a go at writing your own definition of career. What does this mean to you?

> 'I never considered ... how the term career is a lifelong progression. In effect it removes the pressure when it comes to deciding how to choose your career.'

It's all about being strategic

In a world where competition for jobs is fierce, it is vital to be strategic when making career decisions. What is meant by this? Being strategic involves being clear about where you want to get to, and then putting yourself in the best possible position to succeed in that aim. Of course, one of the most difficult aspects of this in relation to career is knowing where you want to get to, particularly when the destination (that is, the labour market) is constantly changing. Getting to a destination is often easier to fathom out when we can use something like a satellite navigation tool; unfortunately, there is no device on the market where you can enter destination unknown and, as if by magic, it will take you there! If you are currently unclear about where your career destination might be, hopefully using this journal in order to reflect on your experiences will help you to see the future more clearly.

Once you have a clearer view of where you might be heading, here are some tips for taking a more strategic approach to your future.

First – find out how you can make progress towards your future. Often there will not be one single route, but a range of options, which can include postgraduate study (for example, master's or doctoral study or a professional qualification), an internship, a graduate scheme or a job with training.

Second – try and speak to people 'in the know'. If you can, speak to people who are in this area of work already. You can do this by talking to previous students who have done your course and are now working. Many universities have strong links with their alumni and should be able to put you in touch with relevant people. You could also make contact with people via social media, such as LinkedIn. This helps you to gain an insider's view rather than relying on second- or even third-hand information.

Third – consider what suits you best and where you will thrive. It is a mistake to assume that what is right for other people will be right for you; always beware of people who say things like 'if I were you I would ...' or 'I did it this way and this way is best'. People vary; for example, some find that their first degree is all they want and after graduation they are ready to have a change and cannot wait to start work. Others have the 'study bug' and want to carry on.

Fourth – it is a good idea to document your progress in a journal like this book. This helps a lot when it comes to interviews for jobs or courses as it makes your thought processes clearer.

What is career happiness?

Career happiness is located on the left-hand side of the CLD Bridge. At first glance, the idea of career happiness might seem fuzzy and intangible and three elements are worth considering. Keyes, Schmotkin and Ryff (2002) describe happiness as subjective and state that it includes those times when we experience pleasure and positive feelings of well-being. They identify two interrelated aspects of psychological well-being that help us to flourish: hedonic and eudaemonic well-being.

Hedonic well-being is the enjoyment of pleasurable moments in life. These give us intense feelings of happiness but are not the norm. The euphoria of finding out that you have succeeded in getting the work placement of your choice is soon followed by the realisation that you want to do well and impress people in order to get a good reference, which brings you back down to earth.

Eudaemonic well-being is an underpinning, longer-lasting but less intense feeling of happiness that comes from such things as being accepting of yourself and others, fitting in, making a contribution, having a sense of meaning and having some control over the realisation of your personal growth and potential.

Another kind of happiness comes when we experience moments of 'flow' (Csíkszentmihályi, 1990) and we are completely 'lost' in the things we are doing. This kind of happiness is about feeling contented and is characterised by a lack of anxiety or longing for things to be different.

Career happiness can involve elements of all three of these types of happiness. It is very much an individual state and varies from person to person. It is also affected by what is happening around us in other parts of our lives.

Career happiness matters because on one level we all spend lots of our time at work, so it really is good if we enjoy it. But it is important on other levels too, as being happy means we are more likely to be optimistic about life, are better able to build positive relationships with those around us and are good to live with. In addition, it is likely that we will have more of a sense of humour and enjoy good health, particularly mental health. However, it is not only our own happiness that is important; gaining happiness at the expense of others can, and indeed should, raise questions of a moral nature. As well as enjoying work, many people also experience happiness by being able to make a contribution to society and by protecting our natural resources.

Try this   Think about what makes you happy. Think of a time when you experienced hedonic well-being. When was this and what caused it? Now think of a time when you experienced 'flow'. Again think about when this was and the reasons for it.

Building career resilience

Career resilience is located on the right-hand side of the CLD Bridge. Being resilient is important in all areas of life, as without it we can become vulnerable and unable to cope with the general demands of everyday life. Resilience can be described as being able to 'bounce back' in the face of setbacks – for example, we experience a negative event and recover from it. Many aspects of resilience are rooted in some of our earliest experiences of the ups and downs of life. We can probably remember falling over as a small child and someone saying to us 'never mind' or 'everything's alright' or 'up you get'. This helps us to recover and carry on rather than giving up. This need to recover from setbacks also applies to our working lives and in this regard career resilience is extremely important, particularly in what can be a volatile labour market.

So how can we build career resilience? First of all, we need to expose ourselves to risk. Unless we are prepared to take some risks, we will never get the opportunity to develop resilience. However, some strong words of caution are needed here; putting ourselves at risk when we have little chance of success is not to be recommended. So, for example, applying for something that we know we have absolutely no chance of getting is foolish and can, if we continue to do this persistently, damage our confidence. On the other hand, we all know that if we constantly 'play it safe', we can begin to feel dissatisfied as we find ourselves saying, 'Well I knew I'd get that anyway'. So it is all about managing risk – not too much and not too little.

Second, we all need support. We need people we can turn to when things do not go the way we want. It is good to choose these people carefully. Ideally they will be people who can help us to think through what we did and why, to help us to move forward rather than those who would just say, 'You didn't get the job? They were mad not to take you!' A mentor (see Theme 1.5) could be an ideal person.

Third, we all need feedback. If we do not get any feedback on the reasons for our lack of success, we are in a vacuum and will not know how to put ourselves in a position to do better next time. Unfortunately, good feedback is not always easy to get and sometimes you will need to be (politely, of course) persistent in asking for it.

In addition, we all need to be ready for change. We all grow and develop as people – jobs and the job market change too; so being able to embrace change and work with it is extremely helpful in building career resilience.

Try this Think about a time in the past when you faced a
disappointment. What did you do in order to overcome this?

Theme 3.5 **Finding your next step to achieve career growth**

Crossing the CLD Bridge involves engaging with career development as we work towards the achievement of career happiness and resilience; this can be described as career growth. If the idea of career is daunting, and you are unclear about the future, it often helps to think about your next steps rather than trying to look a long way ahead, as this lies within our ZPD (Vygotsky, 1978). A placement or internship is an ideal time to research what your next steps could be, and here are some ideas of things you could do to help you to explore this further.

Find out about job opportunities – what job opportunities are there in your organisation? Some organisations advertise their vacancies publicly (particularly online). Try some online research yourself first and then discuss this with someone (for example, your mentor). Try and speak to someone who is involved in recruitment about the range of opportunities that could be on offer. In particular, it is good to know the qualifications they look for in a strong applicant and what the selection process involves.

Find out about training opportunities – many companies and organisations offer training for their staff to help them progress. The training offered to new entrants can help you to see what you could be doing soon.

Find out about opportunities for progression – speak to a manager about what you would need to do in order to progress within the organisation. Remember that in some sectors (for example, media, advertising, IT) staff often move from one company to another in order to progress.

The metaphor of growth is very helpful in relation to career and if we think about how plants grow, we can see some clear comparisons.

Growth in plants	Career growth
Need to be fed and watered	Need activities and experience to enable career learning
Need appropriate sunlight	Need support and encouragement, and can learn more with others than on their own
Need to be pruned	Will experience difficult situations, but this builds resilience
Need fertile ground	Need a positive working and learning environment where risks can be taken without fear of failure, and where constructive feedback is readily available

Growth is often a slow process that happens in sequences. For example, as human beings we learn to crawl before we can walk. Taking things one step at a time and focusing on what we can do next is a positive strategy, and helps to build our confidence.

'I viewed career as something a little daunting and, though I knew I should think about it, I was unsure where to begin.'

Case study : Building career resilience

Sasha graduated with a degree in Sociology and since then has been doing a one-year internship in a small charity that supports homeless people. She is keen to remain in the charity sector and would like to move into a role in administration from where she would hope to progress into an area of management. Sasha has always been a fairly reserved person; at school she was very shy. Her time at university and her internship have both helped to build her confidence.

Sasha's internship is coming to an end fairly soon and so she has been applying for lots of jobs, mostly via key recruitment websites and the press. She has had several interviews but so far has not been successful. Feedback on her interviews has been good; competition is fierce and the phrase she usually hears is, 'You were a strong candidate who came across very well, but there was someone else who was more suited to the role'. When Sasha has asked what she could work on in order to improve, the employers have said, 'Well, nothing I can think of really'. Sasha is growing despondent, so she decides to discuss this with her mentor. During the discussion Sasha's mentor suggests that she needs more feedback and encourages her to try and persist if the same situation arises again.

Soon after, Sasha attends another interview, which she feels goes particularly well. She is very optimistic about the outcome and is hugely disappointed when she is told that she hasn't been successful. She asks for feedback, but again receives a similar message. Because she felt she got on very well with the Chair of the panel on the day of the interview, she decides to persist and asks if there is anything else that she could have done to impress. After giving it some thought, the Chair says, 'Well overall, I suppose you didn't seem quite as enthusiastic as other candidates'.

Sasha has another interview the following week so she goes back to her mentor to discuss the feedback she has received; her mentor says, 'Now I think we're getting somewhere'. They discuss a range of issues such as Sasha's nerves on the day, her self-confidence and how she can sell herself better. Her mentor encourages her to think about wearing a 'metaphorical interview mask' to help her to adopt an interview persona. In particular Sasha begins to see that she needs to put herself forward more strongly and to showcase her genuine enthusiasm for the work. Sasha attends the next interview and gets a job offer.

Theme 4

Skills for working life

This section will:

- ○ Help you to think about how you manage your time
- ○ Enable you to assess how you solve problems
- ○ Help you to think about how you manage your workload
- ○ Encourage you to get to grips with managing your emails
- ○ Help you to think about how you might need to manage your manager.

Being well organised is vital for success on your placement or internship, and good time management is an important skill that is needed in many areas of life. In general, it is something that we need to continually work at; it is dangerous to think that 'we've got it' as it can very easily slip away from us. If you look in any good bookshop or library, or browse online you will find lots of different books on time management because there is no single way of managing time that works well for everyone. If you find an approach that helps you, do use it, but don't become a slave to it, as it may well not work for you forever.

There are several common themes in literature on time management; here are some of them for you to consider.

○ Try to focus on what you want to achieve – this usually involves setting some long-term goals. For example, what do you want to achieve from your time in the workplace?

○ The next step is how you are going to get there – this involves setting some medium- and short-term goals to help you to make progress in the right direction. For example, what do I want to achieve this month, this week and today?

○ Setting priorities – workplaces are busy so it is important to be clear about what you need to do and when. In this respect you need to prioritise what you will do first and so on.

○ Dealing with procrastination – which is often called the thief of time. We all tend to put things off, particularly when we dislike them, find them difficult or are unclear about what we are doing. This means that the time that we had suddenly disappears, or is stolen from us. So developing strategies to overcome this will be important, such as doing the task you have been putting off longest early in the day.

○ Coping with interruptions – there are many things that can easily distract us and waste a lot of our time. The first step is to be aware of them, and then take steps to avoid them or overcome them. For example, if you are distracted by receiving lots of emails, try turning your emails off for a while if you need to concentrate on a specific task.

○ Understanding the difference between the important and the urgent – things that are important help us to achieve our long-term goals (see the first item in this list). Things that are urgent demand our immediate attention and can give us the impression that we need to drop everything and do them straight away. Spending too much time on urgent things can mean that we fail to achieve important things. If we are not careful, the result is that we fail to achieve our long-term goals.

Try this   How do you manage your time at the moment? Where are your strengths? Which areas do you feel you need to work on?

Managing your workload

In all areas of working life it is important to be able to manage your workload and key to this is understanding the difference between the important and the urgent (see Theme 4.1).

Covey (2004a) presents a very helpful model to help us to make this important distinction. This is represented by a square with the following four quadrants.

Quadrant 1 (top left) – things that are both important and urgent. These demand our immediate attention and need to be done now. They usually form key elements of our job.

Quadrant 2 (top right) – things that are important and not urgent. Things here tend to be more long term. Whilst they do not need to be done now, they are very important to us as they help us to achieve our long-term goals.

Quadrant 3 (bottom left) – things that are urgent but not important. These things might appear to be urgent but often are not; mainly this is because they are important to other people, particularly managers.

Quadrant 4 (bottom right) – things that are neither important nor urgent. We can waste a lot of time here, particularly when we feel tired or overloaded.

Many people spend far too much time in Quadrant 1. The consequences of this are that we experience high levels of stress, going from one crisis to the next as everything seems urgent. Lots of time in Quadrant 3 can be equally problematic as we can become slaves to the priorities of other people. Here our own goals and plans can disappear as we constantly seek to please other people. Quadrant 4 is full of procrastination where very little is achieved; this can include constantly checking emails (see Theme 4.4). Covey advocates spending a significant amount of time in Quadrant 2 where we focus on the important things that will help us to achieve our long-term goals. However, it is important to note that important tasks and projects that begin here can move to Quadrant 1 as deadlines loom.

Using Covey's quadrants can be very helpful when we feel that we are losing our focus and allowing our work to get out of control; being able to prioritise our work is at the heart of managing our workload well.

Try this Make a list of things that you feel are in Quadrant 2. Looking back over the past month, roughly how much time have you spent on these things? How might this need to change to ensure that you reach your long-term goals?

'Due to my tendency to doubt my capabilities, I am prone to feeling overwhelmed when faced with a new situation.'

Problem solving

Problem solving is a vital skill at work and is something that we all need to develop. When faced with a problem it is very easy to jump to conclusions, which can often be a mistake. Hicks (2016) offers a very helpful seven-step framework to use when we are faced with problems:

1   Identify the issues – to begin with you need to be clear about what the problem is.

2   Understand everyone's interests – in particular it is important to remember that people have different interests. Hicks emphasises that this step is critical and can easily be missed. What might appear as a problem to one person might be something positive to another. In addition, individuals can have vested interests – things that they want because it will work well for them personally. And others can have hidden agendas – things that they want to happen because it will help them to get what they want in the future; this includes managers.

3   List the possible solutions – there will often be more than one solution to a problem and making a list of these will prevent you from jumping to conclusions too quickly and only considering what appears obvious at first glance.

4   Evaluate the options – this is where you give important thought to the possible solutions. It is important to think about the pros and cons of each in order to begin to reach some conclusions.

5   Select a preferred option or options – on balance decide what will work best. Can any of these options be put together to create a solution that will be supported by most people? But beware of trying to keep everyone happy because this is rarely possible, if ever.

6   Document it – write down how you got to this point. Later on you may well have to justify your decision, and if you don't write it down, you may well forget how you made it.

7   Agree on contingencies and how the decision will be monitored and evaluated – things do not always go to plan so it is important to consider what you would do if that turned out to be the case. Also consider how progress will be monitored so that later you can reflect on whether you made a good decision or not.

Effective problem solving takes time, but probably not as much time as trying to put something right that has gone wrong through a lack of problem solving; so time spent on this is time invested. To solve problems, we often need to slow down and take some time to think things through. Hicks reminds us that while the process involves seven steps, sometimes we will need to go back to previous steps in order to make progress. For example, people's interests might not always be clear, so we may need to go back to step two more than once as these become more evident. You can use Hicks' model on your own, with a colleague or your mentor, or in a small group.

'Interaction with an experienced mentor [helped] to see me through my times of problem solving.'

Managing emails

Emails have become part and parcel of most people's everyday working life. It is obviously a quick and easy way to communicate with people, but if we're not careful it can eat up a vast amount of our time to the detriment of other things that we should be doing. Here are some tips to help you manage emails in the workplace well.

○ Select some specific times in the day when you will send and reply to messages (for example, at the beginning of the day, after lunch and towards the end of the afternoon) and at other times turn your emails off so they don't distract you. Emails can be a serious interruption to your level of concentration and to the flow of your work. It is a mistake to assume that you need to have your email open all the time.

○ Send fewer messages. Choose your messages carefully – the more messages you send, the more you will receive. Often it is easier and quicker to have a conversation with someone in the same office than to send a whole series of emails.

○ Don't be tempted to reply to every message straight away. This can also distract you from your current task and can put unnecessary pressure on the person who has just sent the message. It will probably mean that you will receive another message to follow up. Rather than feeling that you have dealt with something, you can then feel that things are beginning to spiral out of your control.

○ Manage your emails by using a small number of folders. This is a personal thing and will obviously depend on the different elements of your work. Some common folders that people use are 'follow up', 'archive', 'reference' and 'awaiting reply'. Too many folders can make your system cumbersome and you are unlikely to use all of them regularly.

○ Immediately delete messages that do not apply to you. Don't allow these to build up as the number of messages in your inbox will quickly become daunting. If you're not sure whether or not you will need something, put it in your reference folder.

- Avoid clicking the 'reply all' button whenever possible. This means that you will receive fewer messages that do not apply directly to you.
- Only use the 'high importance' button when absolutely necessary. If you get into the habit of using this too much, your colleagues will not be able to tell when a message from you really is important.
- Be mindful of when you send emails. Receiving emails that have been sent in the middle of the night or at the weekend can put the recipient under pressure. If you are worried about forgetting to send a particular message, save it to your drafts or outbox. You can then be sure to send it at an appropriate time.

You will also need to find out about the email policy of the organisation where you are doing your placement or internship. For example, in some organisations all emails are kept and stored for future reference (for example, in relation to contract compliance and customer service). If a client makes a complaint, it is vital to have evidence to show how this was addressed. Be careful about using your personal email at work; some organisations ask staff not to use their personal accounts, not to use social media or not to browse the internet during the day other than for work purposes. Others are much more flexible; if in doubt, be sure to ask.

Try this

How do you manage your emails? If you haven't done so already, make a list here of some key folders for your email system, set them up and start using them.

Theme 4.5 Managing your manager

At first sight this might seem a somewhat strange topic. You might think that it is a manager's job to manage people – not to be managed. However, the working relationship you have with your manager will probably be one of the most important relationships you will have at work. Making sure that you have a strong working relationship with your manager will be vital to your success and development. Here are some tips on building a good relationship with your manager.

○ Accept that they have been given responsibility to supervise your work and always respect that. Even if you do not like them or agree with everything they say, they will write your reference or placement report and you want it to be a good one!

○ Remember they are human and can make mistakes. Managers need support too and an offer of help when they appear to be under a lot of pressure will usually be very well received.

○ Study their management style and observe what makes your manager happy; try to do more of this. This is not the same as 'crawling' or 'sucking up' to your manager; this can make you very unpopular with your colleagues.

○ Never complain about your boss behind their back. Managers will often ask people in their team for feedback on new people and you want this to be positive.

○ Always keep your promises and deliver. If you say that you will do something, be sure to do it. If it turns out that something is difficult or taking longer than you anticipated, be sure to let your manager know in good time and never try to cover it up. New deadlines can sometimes be negotiated or extra help can be offered so that a deadline can be kept.

○ If you are having difficulty prioritising your workload, discuss it with your manager. They will be able to help you to know what you need to do first. This is not an admission of weakness but is a strength, particularly in the early days of a placement or at very busy times.

○ Learn when you need to say no and always do so politely. There is a popular saying in time management literature: 'If you need something doing, ask a busy person.' Most people want to perform well at work, but if we're not careful, we can quickly become the 'go to' person. I have often called this 'punishment for good performance'. Phrases such as 'I won't be able to do that until ...' or 'I have X, Y and Z to do – which do you feel is the most important?' can be very helpful. In particular, be sure to speak to your manager if at any point you begin to feel overloaded.

○ If your manager is difficult to work with, remember that they are human. The pressures that come with management responsibilities can be great, and it could also be that they are having difficulties outside of work.

Case study : Self-management

Katy is on a summer internship in the Human Resources department of a large finance company. She is settling in quite well but soon begins to realise how busy the department is. The demands are high and Katy is expected to work quickly and efficiently, particularly when it comes to responding to queries from applicants and managers of various departments. As a result, she soon begins to feel overwhelmed; Katy's manager sees what is happening and arranges to have a discussion with her about it.

During their discussion her manager suggests a number of strategies to help her to cope with the volume of work and asks her to think about which ones might help. As a result Katy decides to focus on the following three areas.

1   Emails – Katy receives a large number of messages and she feels that her inbox is now unmanageable. She spends a lot of time looking through it to try and find things she needs. She decides to make a concerted effort to reduce it by spending one hour each day putting messages that she needs to keep into folders. With her manager's approval she also turns her email off at particular points during the day to help her to concentrate on other things, such as making arrangements for recruitment days.
2   Diary management – Katy has become forgetful; because of the large volume of work she simply cannot remember everything she has to do. She decides to use her electronic calendar to help her to plan her time more effectively and begins to use alerts to remind her of things she feels she might forget, such as telephone calls she needs to make at particular times.
3   Making lists – Katy starts to use lists to keep herself on track with large tasks that she needs to complete. She realises that she gets satisfaction from being able to cross things off her lists. This helps her to feel motivated and she begins to see that she is making progress.

Before too long Katy feels that she is coping much better with the volume of work. Her manager is pleased and encourages her to attend the next time-management course in order to add to her repertoire of skills.

Theme 5

Effective communication

This section will:

- ○ Help you to think about what constitutes professional behaviour
- ○ Enable you to understand the importance of fostering good relationships with colleagues
- ○ Explain the term 'assertiveness' and discuss its importance in your development
- ○ Help you to think about your social relationships at work
- ○ Stress the importance of keeping in touch with your tutor at university, particularly if you are experiencing difficulties.

Theme 5.1 Professional behaviour

Behaving in a professional manner is something that all employers expect. But what does this actually mean? Here are some important pointers.

- Working hard and always giving your best – everyone will make mistakes and nobody gets everything right all the time. However, employers know when people are working hard and trying their best.
- Be ready to learn – as a university student in the workplace you will not be expected to know everything. Employers are usually very happy to support people who want to learn. When there is something you don't know it is much better to ask questions. Pretending you know is a sure-fire way of coming unstuck sooner or later.
- Always be punctual – everyone can be late occasionally for good reasons but being late persistently gives a very bad impression. Always find out exactly where you are going and allow more time than you need to get there just in case. If you know you are going to be late and cannot avoid it, let someone know what is happening so they know when to expect you. This is always much better than just turning up late.
- Always take a positive approach – people who complain are not good to work with and a positive attitude goes a long way in building good relationships at work.
- Be ready to help – work can come in peaks and troughs and if you can see that a colleague is very busy and you aren't, offer some help.
- Never take the credit for something you haven't done; people understandably get very upset if another person takes the credit for something they have done.
- Always dress appropriately for the organisation – if you are unsure at any point, it is always easier to 'dress down' in a situation (for example, by removing a tie or formal jacket) than to 'dress up'. Don't forget you can always ask a colleague for advice. Be comfortable in what you wear as you will then be able to relax and perform well.

○ 'Mind your language!' – try to speak to people appropriately at all times and bear in mind whom you are speaking to. For example, in a customer service setting you will speak differently to customers depending on their level of understanding of a product. You will probably speak differently again with colleagues and again with managers. Remember, nobody likes to be patronised or 'blinded with science'.

○ Always respect others – in any organisation you will work with a range of people and, unlike your friendship groups, you will work with people you would not ordinarily choose to mix with. Be prepared to work well with people who are different from you and even those you do not like.

Fostering good relationships with colleagues

As soon as we start work we realise that we spend a lot of time in the workplace. Enjoying our time there becomes very important and having good working relationships with our colleagues definitely makes our time at work more enjoyable and productive. But these benefits do not happen automatically and developing them takes time. Here are some ways in which you can do this.

○ Work on your people skills – many people are far too quick to speak and are reluctant to listen. As a result, they go into situations 'feet first' and can upset people before they realise it. Overall being slow to talk and quick to listen is a much more helpful approach.

○ Make time for people – be sure to take some time to get to know those you are working with. The best times for this are during breaks and before and after meetings. Arriving for meetings ten minutes early will not only show you are punctual and keen, but will also give you opportunities to speak to your colleagues more informally. Do not spend lots of time chatting idly and interrupting the work of others and be sure to manage your boundaries carefully.

○ Work on your levels of emotional intelligence, or quotient (EQ) – as distinct from your intelligence quotient (IQ). Our EQ means that we are in tune with our emotional reactions to people and situations (Goleman, 1996). It also means that we can see when others are having an emotional response, for example when they appear angry, frustrated or anxious. Recognising this in ourselves and in others means that we are in a better position to ask for support or to offer it.

○ Appreciate others – always be courteous and thoughtful; a thank you or positive comment such as 'That was a tricky situation and I felt you handled it really well' will do a lot to build positive working relationships.

- Mutual respect – remember that people are different and will not always agree with you. At times compromise will be needed and occasionally it is okay to agree to disagree.
- Avoid gossip – gossip can be a sure way of destroying working relationships. If you are having difficulties, try speaking to the person directly about it. If you don't feel able to do this, speak to your mentor first who may well be able to mediate in the situation. Also, try to avoid office politics.
- Be positive – people much prefer to talk with someone who is positive rather than a person who is continually complaining. Aim for a reference that says, 'X was a pleasure to work with'.

'This will allow me to develop my emotional intelligence ... and find meaning in the work I am doing that can be applied to my future ambitions.'

Try this

Think about your own working relationships and the people you get on well with. What are the factors that make these relationships successful? Now think of those people you would like to get on better with. How might you be able to improve these working relationships?

Assertiveness – what it is and why it matters

In order to function well at work, we need many skills, and assertiveness is certainly one of them. As human beings, when we encounter difficulties our instincts tell us to react with a 'flight' or 'fight' response. As a result, we can be:

- Passive – this is our 'flight' response. It means that we allow other people to get their own way and to 'walk all over us'.
- Aggressive – this is our 'fight' response. We know we need to stick up for ourselves and might even harm others in the process.
- Passive aggressive – this is also a 'fight' response but it is much more subtle. Here we resist indirectly and avoid confrontation; this is manipulation.

Many people are confused about what being assertive means and assume that it is about standing up for yourself and getting your own way. Often this has more in common with being aggressive than being assertive. Lindenfield (2014, p. 3) defines assertiveness as:

> behaviour which helps us to communicate clearly and confidently our needs, wants and feelings to other people without abusing in any way their human rights.

In order to be assertive we need to maintain a balance between our rights or the things that we are entitled to, and our responsibilities towards others. This involves:

- Knowing what our rights and responsibilities are and not allowing one to dominate the other
- Being honest
- Being prepared to express our feelings and views
- Asking for what we want (but not in a demanding way)
- Showing respect for others
- Communicating in a direct way
- Being prepared to speak up for what we know to be right and fair.

Assertiveness is often linked with issues of self-confidence and many of us can think of situations where we would like to be more assertive. But remember that being assertive is also a choice and not necessarily relevant to every situation you may face.

'I know I have a genuine fear of failure.'

Try this Think of some situations in your workplace where you would like to be more assertive. Now think about how you could express your position in a more assertive way.

Social relationships at work

It is always good to get on well with the people you work with, and over time it is likely that some of these people will become your friends. Having friends at work is important as it makes us feel happier and also makes us better at our jobs. If you are a friendly and fairly outgoing person, you won't find it too difficult to make friends in the workplace. However, there are also some pitfalls to avoid.

- It is a mistake to think of your manager as your friend; no matter how well you get on with them, they still have responsibility over your work. They will undertake your reviews and assess your performance; in many situations they will make decisions about your pay and write your reference. In particular, always use social media and text messaging carefully when communicating with your manager. Someone told me recently that they sent a text message to their manager and without thinking put an 'x' at the end of it! They quickly apologised.

- We all spend a lot of time at work and as a result meet people that we have a lot in common with. So it is not surprising when personal relationships start to flourish. However, always bear in mind what it would be like at work if you then broke up – you may then have to spend more time with that person than you would like to! It is usually best to be cautious for a while before becoming involved with someone you work with.

- Having lots of friends at work could be distracting and potentially can cause conflict between people. It is important to remember not to ask someone to do something just because they are your friend. We expect friends to support us and things can become difficult when for good reason a friend feels they cannot do so. Like personal relationships, friendships can break down too.

- Many workplaces have social activities and it is good to go along to these, as they provide a great opportunity to get to know people better. You might also meet people from different departments, which can be useful. However, whenever alcohol is involved remember the golden rule: it's fine to drink, but never get drunk. At social occasions you never know who you might be speaking to and certainly if you are in conversation with the Chief Executive you want to be able to remember what you said! Always remember your reputation is at stake.

Social relationships in the workplace are extremely important; it is particularly important to be known as a likeable person who is good to be around. Many employers emphasise that they look for 'nice people' when they are recruiting, so this will be key when it comes to increasing your chances of being offered a job and something that you will want to put across in job interviews.

Keeping in touch with your tutor at university

If you are undertaking a placement as part of your degree, it will be particularly important to maintain some contact with your personal tutor. Before your placement begins it is a good idea to find out how your tutor would like you to do this; email is by far the most common and easiest method. This is important in two particular areas.

First, if your placement is assessed, your tutor may want to visit you. The organisation of the visit is usually your responsibility and your tutor may well want to spend some time eliciting feedback from your mentor or manager as well as spending some time with you. Even if they do not want to visit it is important to remain in communication with your tutor from time to time to be sure that you are meeting the placement requirements.

Second, contact with your tutor is vital if you feel your placement is going wrong in some way. Always contact your tutor first before leaving a placement prematurely. Even if you are really unhappy and things seem impossible, sometimes things can be done to improve the situation and your tutor will be in a stronger position to do this than you are.

Supportive tutors are always keen to hear from students and to know how they are getting on in the workplace. But always remember busy tutors do not want hundreds of messages! It is also a good idea to keep in touch with your fellow students so that you can offer one another mutual support. Placements and internships can be very challenging times when you can feel anxious and even overwhelmed by the number of new things to learn. Sharing experiences with others who are in a similar position can be very reassuring. It can also help you to see your way out of potentially tricky situations.

Try this

If you haven't had any contact with you tutor since starting your placement, why not compose a short message here to let them know how you are getting on?

Case study : Assertiveness

Jatinder is doing a summer internship in a busy media agency and is keen to learn as much as possible. However, he finds that because people are so busy they do not have much time to explain things. As a result, sometimes he finds that he has too much to do and often is not quite clear about what is expected. At other times he feels he does not have enough to do even though everyone around him is very busy, and often he feels that he is only given very basic tasks, such as photocopying. Jatinder decides to talk all this through with his mentor.

Jatinder's mentor listens to what he says and they begin to discuss his apparent lack of confidence around more senior members of staff. Jatinder soon realises that he reacts to situations with a strong 'flight' response. He wants to become more assertive and his mentor asks him to list the rights and responsibilities he feels he has as an intern. Jatinder writes the following:

Rights
- To have a fulfilling internship that will help me in my future development
- To have a variety of tasks to complete to maintain my interest
- To be respected for what I can offer to the organisation
- To ask for things that will help me to develop (for example, training).

Responsibilities
- To speak up when I don't understand what I need to do and to ask people to explain things more clearly
- To work hard and try to learn quickly
- To offer to help others and ask for more work at quieter times
- To be able to say no when I feel I am becoming overloaded with work
- To treat other people with respect and to recognise when they are too busy to spend lots of time with me.

Following a further discussion with his mentor, Jatinder decides to make an effort to talk to more senior staff in order to build positive working relationships with them.

Theme 6

Learning from feedback

This section will:

- ○ Help you to understand what makes good and bad feedback
- ○ Help you to think about the different settings where you can receive feedback
- ○ Introduce you to the Johari Window model for feedback and self-disclosure
- ○ Enable you to devise some steps to ensure that you get good feedback to help you to progress
- ○ Help you to think about how to prepare for a review meeting.

What makes good feedback?

Good feedback is vital for your growth and development in the workplace. Not all feedback is good feedback, and so it is important to understand and recognise it when given.

Good feedback is:

○ Motivating
○ Honest
○ Respectful
○ Specific
○ Focused on behaviour that can be changed
○ Timely
○ Limited in amount – there is only so much feedback that anyone can cope with at any one time
○ Clear and clarified if necessary, to avoid misunderstandings
○ Focused on positives with some points for further development to enable the person to make progress
○ Helpful and supportive
○ Offered to enhance your development.

Good feedback is not:

○ Hurtful
○ Accusatory
○ Undermining
○ Judgemental
○ Simply personal
○ Too much to take in at once
○ Vague and woolly
○ Only focused on negatives.

Understanding what makes good and bad feedback is very important as it helps you to process it when you receive it. Because not all feedback is good, you should always examine it in order to discern its validity.

When trying to identify good feedback, understanding the model of the 'praise sandwich' can be helpful. This involves starting with some positives, and then focusing on some areas for development or things that could be done better and finishing with a summary of the positives. It is very difficult for someone to move forward in their development if they only receive negative messages. Such messages often start with words like 'but'. Phrases such as 'and instead you could' make feedback much more positive and, thereby, motivating; everyone needs positive points to build on.

Like many other approaches, the 'praise sandwich' has its critics. So, when it becomes obvious, you can either focus on all the criticism and forget the praise, or do the opposite and focus only on the praise and fail to hear any criticisms. If there is too much praise, you can get the impression that everything is okay when this might not be the case. This is an easy trap to fall into if managers need to give you some challenging feedback at any point. If there is too little praise, it can be seen as tokenistic and seem insincere, in which case you are likely to ignore it. Feedback that involves praise followed by development points, using words such as 'as well as' and 'you could develop this by ...', will be constructive, supportive and developmental.

Feedback offered in the form of the 'praise sandwich' boosts confidence, builds self-esteem and helps you to see where you can improve. Good managers want to receive feedback as well, and using the 'praise sandwich' is a good way of doing this if you are ever asked to do so.

Try this When you next receive some feedback, listen for the 'praise sandwich'. Was there any evidence of this? If not, how could it have been used?

Where you can get feedback

We have already established that feedback is an important element of your development in the workplace. Eraut (2006) describes the following four different situations in which feedback can occur.

○ Immediate and in situ – feedback that happens during or immediately following an experience and is given by a colleague or someone who witnesses the event. It is usually specific and often focuses on the factors that influenced the particular situation, which can easily be forgotten later.

○ Informal conversations away from the workplace – feedback can be intentional or more ad hoc and can depend on the learning culture within the organisation.

○ Mentoring and supervision – more formal feedback related to performance, where the mentor or supervisor may not necessarily have direct opportunities to observe the work.

○ Appraisal – more formal and less frequent feedback, which relates to the achievement of goals and objectives set previously.

Eraut is clear that receiving feedback will not always be a positive experience and in fact at times it can even be distressing. However, it is vital for professional development as without it we operate in some kind of vacuum. Here we can deceive ourselves into thinking such things as, 'Well, I thought what I did was okay', or 'I did the best I could', or 'I must have misunderstood what was needed. If someone had explained things better, I would have known what to do'. He also points to the need to use feedback, rather than simply receiving it. This highlights the importance of making a choice: listening, taking stock and acting on feedback when we feel it is justified and appropriate. Engaging in the feedback process means that we will be able to learn from the experiences of others. This could alter our perceptions and help us to begin to see things from the perspective of others as well as from our own point of view.

The Johari Window

When considering the importance of feedback, an understanding of a model called the 'Johari Window' can be helpful. The model was developed by Joseph Luft and Harry Ingham and it can help us to gain useful insights into how we relate to other people. This can give us greater self-awareness in relation to how we communicate with others in a group.

The Johari Window (Luft, 1984) is a square-shaped window with the following four panes.

○ Open (top left) – things that we know about ourselves that others also know

○ Blind (top right) – things that others know about us that we do not know

○ Hidden (bottom left) – things that we know about ourselves that others do not know

○ Unknown (bottom right) – things that no one knows.

The model shows how feedback and self-disclosure can help us to gain greater self-awareness. Being open to feedback and engaging in receiving it will enable you to become aware of those things that others know about you, but you do not necessarily know about yourself. Similarly, being willing to disclose things to others will help them to get to know you better. In both instances, such actions mean that the Open area, where things are known, becomes larger as the Blind and Hidden areas become smaller.

Giving feedback and receiving it, along with self-disclosure, always involves an element of risk, so it is important that it is carried out in an atmosphere of trust. Some people argue that the overall goal is to expand the Open area as much as possible. However, it is important to remember that it is certainly possible to be too open and to disclose too much (see Theme 10.4 in relation to social media). In the workplace it is appropriate that some things remain in the Hidden area – for example, personal issues that you might not want your employer to know. Always remember that some things are disclosed more appropriately only to a friend or relative.

Try this   Ask your mentor and some close colleagues for some feedback on your progress. What did this reveal to you about things that were in your Blind area – things that you do not know about yourself but others do?

How to get the feedback you need

In busy workplaces getting feedback can be difficult because it can be time consuming, but you need it if you are going to develop and reach your full potential. Many people do not know how to elicit the kind of feedback they need, so here are some pointers.

- Be aware of the kind of feedback you are looking for. For example, do you need feedback on a particular project or on certain aspects of your work? Do you need some praise in order to feel more encouraged and supported at work? Or do you need to know more about your key areas for development? When you know what you are looking for, don't be afraid to ask for it – politely of course!

- Ask for feedback sooner rather than later. It is usually easier and less time consuming for someone to give feedback straight away or as soon as possible after an event. Feedback does not always have to be given in a formal meeting scheduled beforehand. Asking to meet for a coffee and a chat is acceptable in many working environments.

- Ask some specific questions. If you ask for general feedback, a good manager will ask you to be specific about what you would like the feedback to focus on.

- Ask for examples. Sometimes the feedback given can be very general; for example, 'I think you could be more assertive'. In an instance like this you need to ask for examples of times and situations where you could have been more assertive and suggestions of how you might achieve this in the future.

- Ask a variety of people. Your colleagues can also give you feedback in addition to your manager, as well as your clients and customers. This way you get a range of different perspectives on your performance at work.

As discussed previously, receiving feedback is not always easy and, generally speaking, the more you receive, the easier it gets. So try not to hesitate or procrastinate, and be sure to ask for feedback often. That way there will be fewer surprises, you will show commitment to your development and your progress will be enhanced.

Try this   Think about the kind of feedback you need for your development. Write some notes to discuss with your mentor.

'Learning will be even stronger if it is done with the help of someone else. A coach, mentor or teacher, who can help us ask those difficult questions and challenge us to look deeper.'

Preparing for a review

At some point during your time in the workplace you will probably have a review meeting about your performance. This will be an in-depth discussion about all aspects of your work and could be with your manager, mentor or a senior colleague. It will be important to prepare well to ensure that it is beneficial for your development. Understandably managers can be very unhappy if people do not plan, as this can give the impression that they do not take the review process seriously. Here are some guidelines for planning for your review meeting.

○ Evaluate yourself honestly. Be clear about your strengths and areas for development. A good review meeting is not only about expecting praise or about 'defending your corner'. It is about learning and development.

○ Set yourself some goals for the coming weeks or months and be ready to discuss them. This is much better than expecting a manager to set these for you and then being taken by surprise.

○ Write some notes beforehand and remember to take these into the meeting with you. In particular write down any specific questions you want to ask and be prepared to discuss them. A question such as 'What do you think I can learn next?' will help you to see the way ahead and will highlight any further training you might need.

○ Don't be afraid to take notes during the meeting. This shows you are taking the process seriously and they will be useful to refer to afterwards as a reminder of things you have agreed to do.

○ Find out if you need to complete any specific paperwork. Large organisations often have paperwork for review meetings that you and the reviewer need to complete. This might involve completing a self-appraisal and sending it to the reviewer by a set time before the meeting. Be sure to find out when the reviewer needs it and to meet the deadline.

○ Lastly, be sure to have a review. In large organisations this kind of meeting will probably happen as a matter of course, but in smaller organisations this is not always the case. If you have been in an organisation for a while and no one has talked about a review meeting, be sure to raise it and ask for one. This shows you have initiative and that you are taking your time in the workplace seriously.

Review meetings should be helpful and informative for both parties. It is important to be open-minded and to listen well so that you hear what is being said and act appropriately on any feedback you are given. Be sure to follow up on any agreed action points, being particularly careful to meet any deadlines set.

'I am going to have to be very self-aware and ensure that I keep focused on moving forward.'

Case study: Lack of feedback

Abdul is studying for a degree in IT and Business Systems and is on a six-month placement in the IT department of a large college. He has been there for six weeks and is unsure about how he is progressing. He still feels confused about how the college is structured and how he is meant to be spending his time. The staff in the department are extremely busy dealing with technical issues, and he feels he is getting very little feedback. Because the staff have very little time, their feedback tends to be quite sharp and negative; he is getting the impression that he needs to work more quickly. Abdul decides to raise this with his manager and beforehand prepares some points that he wants to raise.

When he explains the situation, Abdul's manager is apologetic and admits that Abdul has been 'thrown in at the deep end'. She asks Abdul to say what kind of support and feedback he would like. Referring to his notes, he asks for an induction session, where someone can explain the structure of the college, the role of the IT department and his place within it. Abdul's manager thinks that a mentor would be a good idea and asks him to think about who might fulfil this role – someone he gets on well with and who could support him. They discuss how Abdul can get feedback from staff in the department and his manager suggests asking people for this at appropriate times, such as during breaks and after team meetings. She encourages him to ask them for examples of things he has done well as well as things that he can work on. They also book a review meeting in six weeks' time, at the half-way point of his placement, to review his progress and make an action plan for the final three months. She asks Abdul to bring some SMART goals along with him to the review meeting and to think about his further training needs.

Theme 7

Understanding organisations

This section will:

○ Help you to understand aspects of organisational culture

○ Enable you to see what kind of team player you are

○ Help you to recognise different organisational structures

○ Introduce you to organisational ethics and values

○ Help you to think about the dos and don'ts of hot-desking.

Organisational culture

Organisational culture is an abstract term and is often referred to as 'the way we do things around here'. It is based on the values and beliefs that people share and guides how people behave. Being aware of the culture of the organisation where you are spending time on placement or volunteering is vital to your success. Without this knowledge it is easy to get things wrong without even realising it. Early in my professional life I learned this to my peril at the end of my very first day in a new job. In my previous role I had been used to everyone leaving the office at 5 p.m. (if only it was still like that!) but when I left at 5 p.m. that day I noticed that nobody else did, and I sensed the tension in the atmosphere. The following day I decided to ask the office manager if I had done something wrong. He explained that in that particular setting, everyone left a little later each day, so that they could build up additional time to take a day off. This was a perk that the senior manager used in order to motivate the staff who were working in particularly challenging circumstances. My response was 'why on earth didn't you tell me?' and we laughed about it. Suffice it to say I never left at 5 p.m. again.

Handy's (1993) work on organisational culture has become seminal and he describes four different culture types.

○ Power – this is where the organisation is controlled by one person, or a small group, from the centre. These are the only people who make key decisions and others follow. They delegate tasks to their subordinates and staff are expected to follow. People often feel that they do not have the freedom to express their views or to suggest change.

○ Role – here people in an organisation have a particular role or roles that they carry out. There are usually clearly defined job descriptions and each member of staff is expected to take responsibility for their own area under management supervision and not to stray into the role of someone else.

○ Task – this is very common in many organisations. The focus of staff is on the task being carried out. People are expected to work flexibly, so as one task or project finishes, they pick up the next. Many organisations have moved to a task culture as it is seen as more efficient and effective as things can move more quickly than in a role culture. However, if things move too quickly there can be little time to stop and think.

○ Person – here particular individuals are at the centre and the organisation would not function without them. This would include a general practitioners' (GP) surgery, a dental surgery or a firm of architects. Without the professionals, the organisation would not be viable.

Organisational culture is unwritten and assumed, so you need to pick it up as you go along. Generally you learn by watching what people do and fitting in with their ways of working. Of course if there is a particular aspect that you disagree with, perhaps because it conflicts with your own personal values, this will be a challenge that you might decide you need to address (see Theme 7.3).

Try this   Think about the culture of your own organisation. Which of
Handy's culture types describes this most closely and why?

Team roles

Very few people work completely alone and most work in teams, so an understanding of how teams operate is extremely helpful. In his research at the Henley Management Centre, Belbin (1993) identified the following nine team roles.

○ Co-ordinator – able to get others working to a shared aim; confident, mature and able to delegate

○ Shaper – motivated, energetic, achievement-driven, thrives on pressure, assertive and competitive

○ Plant – innovative, inventive, creative, original, imaginative, unorthodox and good at solving difficult problems

○ Monitor–Evaluator – serious, prudent, critical thinker, strategic, analytical, sees all the options and judges carefully

○ Implementer – systematic, common sense, loyal, structured, reliable, dependable, efficient, practical and turns ideas into action

○ Resource Investigator – extrovert, quick, good communicator, networker, negotiator, outgoing, affable, seeks and finds options

○ Team Worker – supportive, sociable, flexible, adaptable, perceptive, listener, diplomatic, mediator and has a calming influence

○ Completer Finisher – attention to detail, accurate, high standards, quality orientated, painstaking, conscientious, delivers to schedule and specification

○ Specialist – technical expert, highly focused capability and knowledge, driven by professional standards, dedicated to own area of expertise, has knowledge that is in short supply.

A balance of roles is important in any team. If a team is full of Plants and has no Completer Finishers it is easy to imagine that there will be many creative ideas but few will come to fruition. Although many of us have a preference for a particular team role or roles, it is important to remember that in different teams we may play different roles. Like Honey and Mumford's (2000) learning styles, each team role has its strengths which, when overdone, can become a weakness. For example, a Co-ordinator will always walk a fine line between leading effectively to get things done and being seen as bossy and manipulative. A Team Worker is great to work with but can fall into the trap of trying to keep everyone happy. An understanding of team roles will help you to know more about how you work in a team and how others do too.

'I would not just have to be a team player, but also be forward thinking and target focused.'

Try this
Which role or roles do you like to play in a team? At your next team meeting, observe how people operate within the team. Which roles do people seem to play? Are any of the roles missing or in over supply?

Organisational structures

Organisations are structured in different ways to help them to function well and to ensure that staff know who has responsibility for what and who they need to communicate with in particular circumstances. Looking across a large number of organisations, three types of structure are common.

1   Hierarchical or vertical – here the organisation is structured in layers with the Chief Executive or Director at the top and layers of staff underneath (Figure 5). All staff have clear roles and often there is also a role culture (see Theme 7.2). Communication flows 'top down' and 'bottom up' which means it can be slow. Structures such as these are common in large organisations in the public and private sectors.

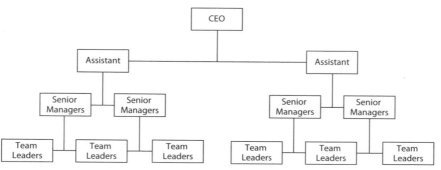

Figure 5 Hierarchical structure

2   Flat or horizontal – in this case there are far fewer layers and staff are organised in teams (Figure 6). This is common in organisations that have a lot of project work, with a team taking responsibility for the work from start to completion. It is also common where the focus is on work with clients or customers. In both instances teams need to communicate well with one another, to ensure knowledge gained from one project is passed from one team to another. Such organisations often have a task culture (see Theme 7.2).

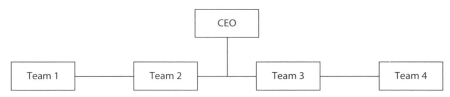

Figure 6 Flat or horizontal structure

3 Matrix – many large organisations have this kind of structure as they
need centralised functions, such as finance and marketing. Figure 7
shows an organisation with a number of teams focused on projects or
clients down the side, and central departments across the top. At some
point, staff in all the teams will need to have contact with people who
have centralised functions. Here there may be a mix of cultures; for
example, a task culture in the teams and a role culture for certain types of
communication.

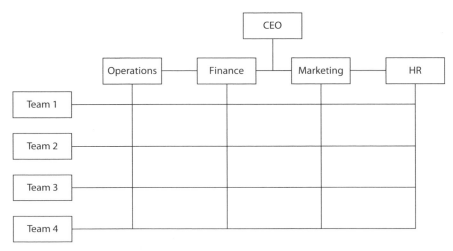

Figure 7 Matrix structure

Having an understanding of how a particular organisation is structured is particularly important for effective communication. So, if the organisation in which you are undertaking your placement or internship has a hierarchical structure, it will be important to communicate with the person at the next level up if a decision needs to be made. Commonly people will refer to this person as their Line Manager. Going over that person's head by speaking directly to the person above them is usually not a good idea, as it can cause offence by giving them the impression that you lack confidence in their ability to manage. In a flat structure communication should flow easily and conversations should be common across teams. However, when decisions need to be made it is important to talk to the team leader or manager. In a matrix structure you will probably have to communicate with different people for different things. Things related to day-to-day tasks will often be discussed within teams, but particular aspects, such as finance, will need to be referred to the specialists.

Try this Get a copy of your organisation's structural diagram. Which type of structure is it and how does it work? If your organisation doesn't have one, try drawing one.

Organisational ethics

Organisational ethics are a set of principles that all staff use to guide their activities and decisions. Ethical leaders and managers use these principles to guide their decisions and they can act as good role models for their staff when they 'practice what they preach'.

Here are some common ethical principles.

○ Honesty – all staff, at every level, are expected to be honest in their dealings with one another, and with clients and customers.

○ Integrity – everyone is expected to apply the ethical principles and aim to produce work of the highest standard.

○ Mutual respect – all staff are expected to respect one another and to value the particular contribution that each person brings.

○ Putting the customer or client first – all staff are expected to put the needs of the customer or client before their own, even if that means staying late to finish a task that is urgent or to meet an important deadline.

○ Adherence to the law – engaging in any activity that could be seen as criminal is definitely out of the question.

○ Loyalty – this involves not doing anything that could bring the organisation into any kind of disrepute or that could aid a competitor.

○ Responsibility for personal action – this means owning up to mistakes and not trying to blame someone else or to 'pass the buck'.

○ Sustainability – many organisations have a desire to preserve the environment and ask staff not to waste valuable natural resources (see Theme 8.5). This can mean such things as only printing and photocopying when absolutely necessary, and recycling whenever possible. It can also include car sharing and being sure to switch off lights when they are not needed.

Ethical codes vary depending on the type of organisation. For example, the code for a medical organisation will be different from that of a financial one. Some organisations, particularly large ones, publish their ethical codes. If you are spending time in a large organisation it is definitely a good idea to ask if you can have a copy of their ethical code; this will often be on the staff intranet and could well be on the external-facing website too. Be sure to read it and, of course, apply it in all circumstances.

'A strong company is one that is well organised, which will use "continuing professional development" to help me to develop my skills, and open up opportunities for me to enhance my career.'

Hot-desking

Many organisations no longer have dedicated office space for particular individuals and ask staff to hot desk. This means that people do not have their own desk or office, but each day sit in a space that is unoccupied when they arrive at work. However, in large organisations, staff teams often sit together whenever possible to aid easy communication.

Hot-desking is now common for a variety of reasons.

○ Technology means that anyone can work from anywhere in a building. Phone lines can be accessed, emails can be sent and Skype calls can be made as long as there is an available network connection. Staff can also work from any location, including from home, and can thereby work more flexibly.

○ It saves money. If desks and workspaces are allocated to individuals, they will be occupied on average for only 50 per cent of the time. This means that higher levels of business rates are paid than are necessary as office spaces are bigger than they need to be.

○ It is environmentally friendly. If office spaces are smaller, they are more environmentally friendly as energy is saved. If staff work from home at least some of the time, they do not travel to work, which means fewer cars on the roads.

If your organisation operates a hot-desking system, it will be important to find out some things in order to be sure that you fit in well; some of this could be described as office etiquette.

○ Are you expected to sit anywhere, or does your team usually sit in a certain area? Either way it will be important not to sit in exactly the same place every day as this can upset people. Inevitably some spaces will be seen as nicer than others (for example, by a window or near the water cooler); it's good to share!

○ Is there a clear desk policy? Hot-desking usually only works if there is a clear desk policy, so be sure to abide by it. Coming in to work and finding an untidy desk strewn with things from the day before is unfair to others and will not win you friends at work.

○ Be clean and tidy. Some organisations provide antibacterial wipes for staff to use on computers and telephones, and hand sanitisers. Be sure to use these regularly. Shared areas, such as kitchens and more informal areas, also need to be kept clean and tidy.

○ Find out about storage space. Most people like to have items at work for their own personal use (for example, pens, notepads). Many organisations have lockers where staff can store these.

○ Find out how long you can be away from your desk. It is easy to irritate people by leaving a desk space unoccupied for a length of time (for example, if you have to attend a meeting) particularly if an office is very busy. Some organisations have a policy of asking staff to clear their desk if they are going to be away from it for more than an hour.

○ Use a desktop computer sensitively. Many organisations allocate laptops for staff to use at work, which can then be taken to different spaces within the office and used when working from home. But if your organisation uses desktop computers, always be sure to lock them when you leave your desk for a short period of time and to log off when you leave. Finding an empty space and then trying to log on to a computer that is either locked or logged on for another user is very annoying!

Jerome is doing a six-month placement in the fundraising department of a children's charity and is keen to fit in well. During the short time he has been in the organisation, he notices some particular aspects of the ways in which people work that he feels are important to follow.

The atmosphere is generally fairly relaxed but people are always busy and do not have lots of time to stand and chat. Jerome quickly becomes sensitive to situations where people need to get their work done and tries not to disturb them. He is also sure to concentrate on his own work in order to perform well. However, it soon becomes clear that Fridays are very different; he notices that people dress more casually and everyone stops for tea and cake at 3.30 p.m. to socialise. By 5 p.m. the office is almost empty and people are making their way home or are off for an evening out. The following Friday he enjoys wearing his jeans for work.

As part of his role Jerome soon begins to become involved in fundraising events. Some of these are formal, high profile and take place in the evening. Staff are keen to attend as they are seen as a vital part of raising large amounts of money for the children and families they are supporting. Jerome decides to buy a good-quality suit from one of the organisation's charity shops to wear at the next key event.

One day Jerome notices on the intranet that the charity encourages staff to spend a week each year volunteering in a setting where they come into direct contact with children. He talks to his mentor about the possibility of spending two days in a local special school and his mentor helps him to arrange it.

Values

This section will:

- ○ Help you to think about what you want from work
- ○ Introduce you to different employment sectors
- ○ Encourage you to think about what kind of organisation you would fit in with
- ○ Introduce you to the idea of a working legacy
- ○ Consider important issues of sustainability.

What do I want from work?

When thinking about your career development, in order to achieve career happiness (see Theme 3.3) it is vital to understand your personal values in relation to work. Different things motivate different people and what is very important for one person can be insignificant for another. Here Schein and Van Maanen's (2013) concept of 'career anchors' is very useful.

Schein and Van Maanen (2013, p. 1) define a career anchor as a 'combination of perceived areas of competence, motive, and values that *you discover you would not give up* if you faced a career decision that would not allow you to fulfil it.' So, a career anchor is made up of things that we believe we can do well, things that we are keen to do, and things that are important to us. The key point that they make is that these are things we would not want to give up; if we were in a job where these could not be incorporated, we would not be satisfied or happy.

Schein and Van Maanen describe the following eight career anchors.

1 Technical expertise – people who want to have a high level of specialism in a particular area (for example, engineering, teaching) and would not want to move into a management position.
2 Managerial – these people are generalists who like to lead, and to move around into different areas of work.
3 Autonomy/independence – people who dislike rules, and want to work independently and have responsibility for their own work.
4 Security/stability – these people dislike risk and enjoy being able to identify with an organisation because it makes them feel safe and secure.
5 Entrepreneurial/creativity – people who like creating new things (for example, products and services), enjoy seeing a result from their own efforts and often enjoy making money.
6 Service/dedication to a cause – this points to the issue of personal values, where serving others and making a contribution to society are key to someone's motivation.

7 Pure challenge – here it is not the job itself that is important, but the enjoyment of working hard and succeeding, whether it is in overcoming a difficult problem or completing a large project.
8 Lifestyle – people who are keen to integrate work into their lives and to be able to achieve a good work–life balance.

Most people have more than one career anchor and discovering these can be a vital step to finding an area of work that you will enjoy and find fulfilling.

'My values, interests and aptitudes have been influenced by my upbringing; I work hard but value the importance of establishing a career I enjoy and am good at.'

Try this   Looking back at your SWOT/SWAIN analysis from Theme 2.2, which of the career anchors do you most identify with and why? How might this help you when making your career decisions?

Which sector do I want to work in?

Looking at the labour market, very generally there are three main employment sectors.

1 Private or corporate – companies that generate money from goods and services that they sell to make a profit. These companies range from global multinationals to small and medium enterprises (SMEs).
2 Public – organisations that receive their money either directly or indirectly from the government. They include the civil service, local authorities, state-funded educational establishments and health services.
3 Charity – organisations that rely on donations from the public. They can sometimes receive grants from other sources such as the National Lottery and government departments.

All three of these sectors play an important part in our overall economic activity. In addition, there are a growing number of people who are self-employed.

Many roles are available in more than one sector, and the sector you choose to work in could have a profound impact on how satisfied you are at work. For example, if you want to work in finance, you could work in any of the sectors, but the emphasis in the job would be different in each. In the corporate sector the focus would be on making a profit and building the company's financial profile. In the public sector, ensuring the best use of the money available will be central, as well as making sure the books balance and certainly not making a loss. In times of recession this will often mean implementing budgetary cuts. In the charity sector, making sure that money goes to the people who should receive it will be important, as well as ensuring it is not wasted in any way. One example of someone who would be self-employed in this area is a consultant who helps small companies with their finances and other self-employed people with their tax returns.

Understanding your career anchors can help you to think about which sector you will be happy in. For example, if your career anchor is service/dedication to a cause, you might be happier working in the charity or public sector. If it is entrepreneurial/creativity, you might enjoy working in the corporate sector and then become self-employed. If your career anchor is managerial or pure challenge, you could work in any organisation and even move from one sector to another. To make matters even more complicated, the same job in the same sector can be very different depending on the particular organisation or company (see the case study at the end of this section).

When you reach the point of applying for jobs or graduate schemes, there will be no substitute for finding out as much information as you can about the place you are applying to. In order to get a sense of how far their values match your own, be sure to look at their websites, as lots of organisations publish their mission statements. Be ready to be asked about these if you get an interview, as employers want to recruit people who fit with their aims and vision.

What kind of organisation would I fit in to?

Finding out what kind of organisation you will fit in with can be a complex process and it is well worth thinking through some particular issues. Some of these we have considered already, such as the kind of organisational culture that will suit you (see Theme 7.1), how the organisation is structured (see Theme 7.3) and which sector you might prefer (see Theme 8.2). Another key factor in helping you to make this decision will be the size of the organisation concerned and there are many pros and cons to consider in relation to this.

Size of organisation	Culture/Structure	Pros	Cons
Large – employs over 250 people	Role or Task/ Hierarchical or Flat	Wide variety of jobs available. More opportunities for training and development. More opportunities for promotion. Larger teams.	Lines of communication can be slow. Bureaucratic, inflexible and process driven. Can stifle creativity. Slower to give responsibility.
SME – employs fewer than 250 people	Could be any of the four culture types. Could be any of the three structure types.	More variety of work. Smaller teams. More early responsibility. More creativity and flexibility.	Fewer opportunities to specialise. Fewer opportunities for promotion. Lack of some central services.
Small – employs fewer than 20 people	Power or Task/ Hierarchical or Flat	Even more variety of work. Responsibility given even earlier. Knowing everyone you work with. Even more flexibility and creativity.	Might be expected to do anything when it needs doing. Could mean too much responsibility too soon. Fewer formal opportunities for training and development.

It is also important to remember that something that is an advantage for one person could be a disadvantage for another. For example, the formal lines of communication in a large organisation could offer a degree of comfort and security to someone, but could restrict and even stifle someone else. The important question is what will suit you best, and your current experiences will certainly help you with this.

'I am developing my character as well as my skills in order to prepare myself for employment.'

Theme 8.4   When I look back, what will I be proud of?

In Theme 1.2 we looked at goal setting, Covey's (2004a) notion of 'begin with the end in mind' and the importance of being clear about what you want to achieve. In his book *The 8th Habit, From Effectiveness to Greatness*, Covey (2004b) takes this several steps further and discusses the notion that as human beings we have a desire to leave a legacy – something that will become part of our personal history. Covey is clear that our legacy will not, and should not, relate simply to work, as our personal lives are also very important.

Another way of exploring our values and what is important to us is to look ahead and consider achievements during your working life that would make you proud. So imagine you are approaching the end of your working life; what do you hope to have achieved? Of course this will be different for different people, but here are some areas that you could think about.

○ Qualifications – many people go on to undertake further study following their degree. Some continue straight away and others return to study much later on. Some take master's and doctoral degrees, and many opt to study from the wide range of professional qualifications available. Could more study be for you? If so, how much would you like to achieve?

○ Promotion in a particular field of work – some people aim high and, for example, know that they would like to be a Chief Executive or a Michelin star chef by a certain age. Do you have any such aspirations?

○ That 'thing' that you have always wanted to do – some people dream about doing something they have always wanted to do, for example writing a book, swimming the channel, running a marathon, starting a business or taking a creative idea forward to try and develop it. Is there something like this that you can identify?

Having a sense of what we would like to be able to say that we have achieved can give us pointers for the future. It can also help us to be more strategic when making decisions that affect our future. However, this can be difficult if you are still unsure about your longer-term aims. In this instance you could also think about the things that you would regret not doing when you look back. This could give you some important pointers to some of your key interests.

Try this

Imagine it is 10 years from now and your university is holding an alumni event for people who graduated at the same time as you. At the event you meet some people that you have not seen since you graduated. What do you hope you would be discussing in relation to your achievements at work?

Many people are becoming more and more concerned about sustainability issues and want to protect and preserve the environment. Many organisations share these concerns and while you are in the workplace it is good to notice the steps that your organisation is taking in this important area. Here are some pointers.

○ Recycling – many things can be recycled; paper is the most obvious thing but glass, packaging, cups from the coffee shop, cans and plastics can too. Lots of organisations have a range of bins for different things.

○ Smoking – of course this is illegal in public places, including places of work.

○ Energy saving – many offices have lights that turn off automatically when rooms and corridors are not in use. Some organisations only purchase energy from companies that are committed to renewable energy.

○ Paperless offices – some offices aim to use no paper at all, and others as little as possible. Many would say that printing and photocopying should only be carried out when absolutely necessary and should always be done double-sided. Documents can be scanned and saved easily on computers instead of being kept in filing cabinets. Many only use recycled paper when paper is needed.

○ Travel to work – many employers want to encourage people to travel to and from work using public transport and by cycling where possible in order to reduce carbon footprints. If people have to drive, they are encouraged to use park and ride services in order to make city centres less congested. Car sharing is also encouraged and many people now have to pay to park at work. Travelling to meetings is discouraged when alternatives such as video conferencing are available.

○ Drinks – many workplaces have water coolers that supply filtered tap water. These are cheap to run and offer an alternative to bottled water, thereby reducing the number of lorries on the roads transporting water long distances. In their cafés they only sell fair trade and organic drinks.

○ Using local products and services – this can range from using local suppliers to provide the food in the coffee bar to using local engineers when heating systems fail.

○ Using environmentally friendly products – this includes using cleaning products that cause less harm to the environment.

An organisation that takes steps such as these has a real concern for the environment. Whilst on placement it is important to participate in what they are trying to achieve and to respect their aims.

Try this
Does your organisation have a sustainability policy? If so, familiarise yourself with it and make some notes here on how you might apply it.

Case study: Values

Bradley graduated with a degree in Business Studies. During the vacation following his second year he did a summer internship with a finance company in the private sector and following this decided that he was interested in pursuing a career in some kind of management. Bradley had been interested for some time in sustainability issues and after doing some research he very much liked the idea of working in management consultancy. Before he graduated he was successful in gaining a position as a graduate trainee with a company offering management consultancy services. Even though this organisation was also in the private sector, it soon became clear that the ways of working in this organisation were very different from those he had experienced whilst doing his internship. Expectations were very high, which was not a problem in itself, but because of the results-driven culture, staff were expected to stay until tasks were finished, even if this meant working into the night. Bradley found the clash with his own values extremely difficult and so decided to look for another job. After six months he left the organisation and joined another management consultancy that focused on advising businesses on issues of sustainability. In particular, they specialise in helping businesses to find a better work–life balance for their employees as they believe that this helps people to perform better in their jobs, which, in turn, makes businesses more successful. As an organisation they 'practice what they preach' so all staff finish work no later than 6 p.m. Bradley is again working in the private sector, but is now much happier in an organisation that is more in tune with his personal values. In addition, he is working with managers in other organisations that also share his values.

Theme 9

Managing stress and change

This section will:

- ○ Help you to understand more about the concept of transition
- ○ Enable you to notice the signs of stress in yourself and others
- ○ Help you to apply some strategies for managing stress
- ○ Enable you to consider issues of work–life balance
- ○ Encourage you to think about how to build your confidence.

What is transition?

Transition is a term that is used to describe a major change in someone's life from one state to another. It can include such things as bereavement, marriage, divorce and becoming a parent. Graduation and starting a first job would be described as a transition as the level and scope of change are very significant. As well as it being a very different way of life from being a student, it could include relocation; without wishing to sound overdramatic, life will not be the same again. Transition is a process not an event, and it takes time to adjust to the changes that are taking place.

It is common to experience a range of different emotions, including highs and lows, as you go through the transition process. Adams, Hayes and Hopson's (1976) work on transition has become seminal and their seven-stage model describes how many people think and feel during the process.

Stage 1 – Immobilisation. The process is very new and we can have a feeling of being overwhelmed by the enormity of the transition. This means we 'freeze' and do not know what to do next.

Stage 2 – Reaction of elation or despair. If the transition is seen as positive, we feel elated; if we see it as negative, we can have a sense of despair.

Stage 3 – Self-doubt or minimisation. As the impact of the transition becomes clearer, our elation turns to self-doubt and, as our feelings dip, we ask ourselves questions such as 'can I actually do this?' Alternatively, our feelings of despair are minimised, and we tell ourselves things like 'maybe this won't be so bad after all'.

Stage 4 – Acceptance and letting go. This is about accepting that the change is happening and recognising that it won't go away. We start to look forward and begin to let go of the past.

Stage 5 – Testing. As we move on to the new situation, we begin to try out new ways of working and living.

Stage 6 – Search for meaning. This is a period of reflection when we contemplate what has happened and explore what the change means for us.

Stage 7 – Integration. This meaning is internalised and the change is accepted as part of our everyday lives. The new state becomes the norm.

It is helpful to know that these stages of transition show us that we often experience highs and lows over a period of time as we experience change. It is important to know this about ourselves but also for others too, so we can offer support and encouragement to those around us.

We all experience stress at various times and indeed need it in order to perform well at work. Stress is our physical, emotional and mental reaction to any kind of demand that is made on us, or that we make on ourselves. When such demands are made our bodies react by releasing chemical hormones into the blood called endorphins that help us to cope. A good amount of stress is a positive thing, as it energises us and helps us to achieve. However, too much stress is not a good thing. Generally, the word stress has negative connotations and we automatically think of words such as anxiety and pressure – hence the word distress.

Noticing signs of stress in yourself is important. Fontana (2005) highlights the following three groups of symptoms of stress.

1 Cognitive – too much stress affects our thought processes and means that we can find it difficult to concentrate for any length of time, and are easily interrupted and distracted. Our responses slow down and we make more mistakes than we would usually. We organise ourselves poorly because we can no longer assess accurately how long it will take us to do things, and we can become confused and illogical.

2 Emotional – too much stress means that we find it very difficult to relax or 'switch off'; we worry about even little things and generally feel very anxious. Sometimes we can imagine that we are ill and can begin to feel unwell. Things that we feel anxious about become exaggerated in our minds and small task can feel like a mountain to climb. We can become oversensitive or defensive, which might lead to emotional outbursts in situations that we find particularly difficult. In extreme cases we can become depressed and our feelings of self-worth can plummet.

3 Behavioural – too much stress means that we can become disinterested in things that previously we loved doing. We lack enthusiasm, become cynical and lethargic because our energy levels are low. Our regular sleep patterns can change and be interrupted, for example waking up in the middle of the night and not being able to get back to sleep again. We might start to take days off work, ignore information and advice even when it is helpful

and shift responsibilities on to other people. We might begin to look at everything at a more superficial level, and our responses to people and situations can become unpredictable. Our consumption of substances such as caffeine and alcohol can increase and some of our regular habits might change. For example, tidy people might become messy and someone who is caring could become cold and indifferent as other people's issues become too much to cope with.

It is good to recognise high levels of stress in yourself as you will then be in a position to do something about it (see Theme 9.3). It is also helpful to be able to notice signs of stress in others so you can offer support when and where appropriate.

Strategies for managing stress

Many people at work experience high levels of stress and it is important to do whatever we can to try and reduce it. This is not always easy and will again vary from person to person. The key is to find what works for you and to apply it. Be aware also that something might work for a while, and you may then need to change your approach. Here are some ideas of things you can do to reduce your stress levels.

- Time management – go back to Theme 4.1 and look again at how you are managing your time. It might be that you need to make some changes to become more effective again.
- Assertiveness – we can become stressed when we are passive and unable to say no. If you feel overloaded, go back to Theme 5.3 and consider how you can be open and honest, and say no effectively. In the end this is much better than saying yes and failing to deliver.
- Physical exercise – this uses up our excess adrenalin and releases endorphins. It also forces us to take some time out and distracts us from whatever is making us anxious. All exercise is good, so do something that you enjoy.
- Relaxation techniques – most of these involve breathing exercises and relaxing each part of your body whilst lying down. It is commonly accepted that 20 minutes of relaxation equates to two hours of sleep. A simple thing like relaxing in a hot bath can also be very effective.
- Build your support networks – make sure that there are people around you who you can go to for support. Also remember to support them when they are feeling stressed.
- Make some time for yourself – take some time out on a regular basis to do things you enjoy.
- Set yourself some new challenges – do some of the things that you have been wanting to do. These do not have to be big things; it could be reading a particular book or listening to a new album.

○ Avoid unhealthy habits – we can easily crave comfort when we are feeling stressed but things such as smoking, snacking and drinking (including caffeine) can leave us feeling worse in the longer term.

○ Consider some healthy remedies – there is a wide range of these on the market ranging from 'rescue remedies' to herbal teas.

○ Stay positive – remember times when things have gone well and you have been successful and focus on these.

○ Understand what you can and cannot change – spending precious time and energy trying to change things that cannot be changed is time wasted, and is very wearing and discouraging.

There is no single remedy for managing stress, but a range of things to try. If they work for you, do more of them and if they don't, move on to something else. Be willing to share the things that work with those around you, as this could help them too.

Try this   Think about what helps you to manage stress. Make a list here of things that might help you in this area. Why not plan a stress-relieving activity once a week and insert it into your planner?

Work–life balance

A key part of managing stress is having a good work–life balance. In busy workplaces where everyone has access to their work 24 hours a day via technology, it is easy for work to take over our lives. In global companies and services, as one country goes to sleep another wakes up and we can fall into the trap of thinking that we need to do everything now, particularly when things move at such a fast pace. The price we can pay for allowing work to take over is very high, and includes things such as tiredness and exhaustion, poor diet, lack of exercise, anxiety and feeling under constant pressure. In extreme cases this can lead to burn out and even depression. The outcome of all of these is poor performance at work.

Maintaining a healthy work–life balance will be important during your time in the workplace so that you can perform well and get the most from your experiences. Here are some tips to help you.

○ Boundaries – the boundary between work and life outside has become blurred because of things such as webmail, remote desktop working and smartphones. We no longer need to be in our place of work to be able to work. This is a positive thing as it means that we can work from anywhere, including from home, but is negative when it means we slip into the trap of working all the time. Having some clear boundaries will be important for the future and now is a good time to think about them and to start using them. For example, not having your work email on your personal smartphone is a good idea. This should be for your own use and a means of getting away from work. If you sometimes work at home, if possible do this in a separate room. This means you can close the door when you've finished and your work is contained. Be sure to set up your out-of-office message for when you are on holiday and do not be tempted to check emails while you are away. If you know you will be tempted (email can be addictive!) and you have a portable work device, leave it at home.

○ Work smarter not longer – this again relates to the whole area of time management (see Theme 4.1). Time at work can easily be wasted and we all need to review our time-management strategies regularly.

○ Speak up before things get overwhelming – if too much is being expected of you, you need to say so. All employers want their staff to perform well and good employers will want to support those who are finding things tough. Maintain good open communication with your mentor. If you feel that you are spending more and more time at work, keep a log and take this along to your discussion.

○ Take proper breaks during the day – it is well known that we all need such breaks. Take at least half an hour for lunch and avoid the habit of eating lunch at your desk. Ideally get some fresh air, especially if you work in an air-conditioned environment. Even a short walk to a coffee shop can be very beneficial. Overall you will feel fresher when you get back and will not find yourself 'flagging' by about 3 p.m.

○ Make time for family, friends and the things you enjoy – if you feel you have no time for these, you are too busy. Remember, ultimately the only time we have is the time we make.

Many people have concerns about their work–life balance. Most of us will have to work for more years than our parents and grandparents, so it is important to address this important issue. Applying some of the strategies listed above should help you to keep an eye on this key area.

> 'I am keen to learn as much as I can … although I am aware that I would have to be mindful not to allow my work to become all-consuming.'

Try this Observe the people around you. How successful are they in maintaining a good work–life balance? You could also discuss this with your mentor.

Building confidence

Confidence is an intangible thing; it can be difficult to build and easy to lose. Having confidence in yourself is something that develops over time as you gain more experience, but of course, no one likes a person who is overconfident and brash. Confidence is an important aspect of resilience (see Theme 3.4) and if you feel that you need to gain more confidence in the workplace, here are some things you can try.

○ Be prepared to step outside your 'comfort zone' and take some risks – if we only ever do things that we know we are confident doing, we will not cope well with tasks that are new and our resilience will be low. But be sure to manage the risks by not doing things that are far too difficult, so that you can achieve career growth (see Theme 3.5).

○ Always say at the time when you don't understand something – many people are afraid to do this because they see it as expressing a weakness. This is far from the truth; saying that you are not clear, or do not know how to do something, shows you are willing to learn and this is a strength.

○ Follow the 5 Ps – Prior Planning Prevents Poor Performance. In other words, 'to fail to plan is to plan to fail'. Always prepare whenever you can, as you will then put yourself in a better position to succeed, which will boost your confidence.

○ Get used to accepting compliments – when people praise you for things you have done, give yourself a metaphorical 'pat on the back' and never do yourself down with phrases such as 'it was nothing' or 'anyone could have done that'.

○ Dress the part – there is a lot of truth in the phrase 'if you look the part you feel the part'. Wearing the right clothes in a situation can help you to feel more confident. Try not to underdress or overdress and always feel comfortable in what you wear.

○ Be proactive – if at all possible make sure that you get the experience you would like. Again a good relationship with your mentor will be vital as they will probably hold the key to this.

○ Don't be a 'wall flower' – standing on the sidelines is appropriate in some situations but not all the time. As you gain more experience, speak to others you don't know in the workplace. A social event can be a good place to practice before you do this at a meeting.

Remember confidence comes through experience, and overall the more you do the easier it gets. But remember also that everyone has 'knock backs' and bouncing back from them is a vital part of building resilience.

'I was full of self-doubt, which is a common barrier to career development.'

Try this

Speak to someone this week who you have not spoken to before. Look out for new people as they will also be looking out for people to get to know. Make some notes here on how this went.

Case study: Work–life balance

Alisha is on placement as an administrator in a busy orthopaedic outpatients department in a large hospital and is finding her work increasingly stressful. She decides to discuss her situation with her mentor where she explains some of the things she is experiencing. She explains that she feels very tired quite a lot of the time. Because of the volume of work, she often stays late and then finds it very difficult to switch off from work when she gets home. She finds herself thinking about all the things she needs to get done the next day, and then finds it difficult to get to sleep. This means she feels even more tired and when she does finally get to sleep, she then often wakes up with a headache.

Alisha's mentor helps her to identify some strategies to help her. They decide that there is a danger that work is taking over Alisha's life, and that it would be good for her to establish some boundaries between her work and home life. Alisha removes her work email from her smartphone, and when at work she decides to check her emails at specific times of the day rather than checking them constantly. She asks one of her close friends to meet with her each week to do something they enjoy, and she decides to swim once a week. Over time Alisha begins to feel the benefits of what she is doing and her work–life balance starts to improve.

Theme 10

Networking

This section will:

○ Discuss what networking is and why it matters
○ Help you to begin to map your networks
○ Discuss how you can extend your networks
○ Help you to understand the need for a positive digital profile
○ Help you to consider the possibility of becoming an entrepreneur.

What is networking and why does it matter?

Your network is the number of people that you have contact with, and as you gain more experience, your network will grow. Your network will include people from the following areas.

○ Family
○ Friends
○ Neighbours
○ Colleagues in your workplace
○ People you have worked or studied with in the past
○ People you have contact with at meetings
○ Clients.

People in your network are individuals that you have got to know and have begun to build authentic relationships with; they are more than acquaintances.

In relation to career and personal development having a network of people you are in contact with is important for a number of reasons. First, it is well known that many job vacancies that are available are never advertised; they are offered to people who know people. This is often referred to as the informal job market and is hidden. Tapping into your networks will be an important way of making sure you don't miss out on opportunities.

Networking with key people gives you access to a wealth of knowledge and experience. People from different backgrounds have different perspectives and can help you to see things from a range of angles. They can offer support and new insights into situations you are facing. Remember also that connections make more connections, because people know different people. This is how your network grows.

Networking is something we do all the time and can happen anywhere: at work, on placement, when volunteering and in our social lives. It is important to remember that, in general, people want to build relationships with people they know, like and trust; so being approachable, likeable and trustworthy is very important. Nobody will recommend someone for anything unless they are confident in the person, because it means that they put their own reputation 'on the line'.

Networking is sometimes daunting, but remember that you have started already and now is definitely the time to continue.

'I learn new things all the time. I am gaining so much experience in a new field.'

Being in any workplace means that you have the opportunity to start networking and it is a good idea to map out whom you have contact with so that you can make the most of your contacts. Taking a strategic and analytical approach will help you to see which particular relationships will be of most value to you. Here are some steps you can take to map your network; these can be done on a large sheet of paper, or on your tablet or laptop.

Step 1 – start by making a list of all the people you are in regular contact with; remember this includes family and friends as well as people you have met in the workplace. These are people with whom you might have direct contact, for instance face-to-face or over the phone, or indirect contact, for example via email or social media.

Step 2 – rank your top-ten contacts from one (most important) to ten.

Step 3 – put people together into groups and label them. The groups themselves will vary from person to person and need to be relevant to you as an individual. Some examples could be potential employers, support, training ideas and knowledge of a particular sector. Code them by colours to make the groups stand out.

Step 4 – look at the links between groups and which groups contain most of your top-ten contacts. These will be the groups to focus on for effective networking.

Step 5 – now look for the gaps. These are areas that you will want to work on in the future.

Seeing your network in a visual format can help you to appreciate both the number of contacts you have and the areas where you might need more.

Try this   Follow the steps in Theme 10.2 to map out your network. Who are the key people in your network? Where are the gaps?

Extending your networks

Having started to map your networks, you will have begun to see where the gaps are and can begin to consider the people you would like to build new contacts with so that you can extend your network to make it more effective. This might sound like some kind of 'cold calling', or walking up to people and trying to start a conversation without knowing what to expect; all of this can sound quite scary. But rest assured it does not have to be like that and here are some ideas to help you to think about how you can network effectively with more people.

○ If you are not doing so already, consider doing some volunteering. Be sure to target people and organisations that will be able to help you in your future development.

○ Attend some key events where you will be able to meet new people. Consider doing this with someone else as this is often easier than doing it alone.

○ Use your university's alumni network. All universities want to keep in touch with their graduates, so be sure to ask your tutors how you can make contact with people who have graduated recently, say in the last five years. People are always busy but often happy to chat with others about their work, particularly people who are doing the course they used to do.

○ Do some research first. Reading about particular areas of industry and the opportunities available means that you will have more to talk about when you meet new people. This will help you to feel more confident.

○ Consider joining an appropriate organisation. Many areas of work have professional organisations and these are an ideal way of meeting like-minded people and making new contacts.

○ Step out and do it now. It is very easy to procrastinate and this often means that things become much bigger in our heads than they need to be. Remember that the new people you are making contact with are all human beings and the worst that can happen is that you catch them on a bad day.

○ Have a strong social media presence. Make sure that it is professional (see Theme 10.4) and always shows you in a good light.

The idea of extending your network can be scary to start with and most of us are happiest with people we know well. However, the more you network the easier it gets and remember, the rewards can be great.

Try this   Make a list of the new contacts you would ideally like to make in the next month and start contacting them.

Your digital profile

Having a digital profile is now part and parcel of everyday life. Most of us have one and it is important that it says positive things about us and puts us across in a good light. Many employers look at digital profiles as part of their process of recruitment, so at some point you may well need to consider checking your profile and trying to remove things that you would not want a prospective employer to see. You can do this in a variety of ways.

○ Search for yourself online and see what you find. This is as simple as typing your name into a few search engines and looking at what comes up. Be particularly sure to include social media sites.

○ Decide on what you are happy for anyone to see, and things that you would prefer a recruiter or employer not to see. Be sure to use privacy settings where appropriate, but also be aware that this is not foolproof. An employer only needs to say 'didn't you go to that university?' and ask an employee to look for you, and they will probably be able to find you.

○ Think before you post things online. It might be funny when you post photos during a 'big night out' but you might regret it later.

○ It is impossible to control what others post about you on the internet, but if there are things you are really unhappy with, try asking them to remove them or, again, to use privacy settings.

○ Start building up a positive digital presence. The more you do this, the more positive information will appear on the first page when people search for you. Most people do not have endless time to search through pages of 'hits'.

○ Use a professional site such as LinkedIn and be sure to have a professional-sounding email address; if necessary create a new email account specifically for everything related to your future development.

Having a presence online is now part of most people's lives. Making sure that you portray yourself positively is the same here as in every other aspect of life when it comes to your personal and professional development.

Try this

Plan a time when you will start to clean up your digital profile. Make some notes here on how you will approach this. Why not agree to do this with some friends so you can work together?

Theme 10.5 Becoming an entrepreneur

Following graduation some people decide to try and take an idea forward in order to build a successful business themselves. Most entrepreneurs would say that this is difficult and risky, but potentially very rewarding. The idea of being your own boss can be very attractive and is something that an increasing number of people do at different points in their working lives. Many have the idea of running their own business, but far fewer people actually do it. Many start by working for a company (for example, a start-up) or organisation, and then striking out on their own later.

If starting your own business is something that you feel you would like to do, here are some ideas to help you to get started.

- Some colleges and universities run short courses in entrepreneurship that could be worth investigating. This should give you an accurate picture of what is involved and the process you would need to follow to get started; this often includes how to devise a business plan. Be sure to find out about these opportunities whilst you are still studying as there could be free seminars available that you can tap into.

- Organisations such as The Prince's Trust offer help and support to young people who want to start their own businesses. This includes linking people up with a mentor who can offer invaluable advice and support from their direct experience.

- Financial acumen will always be important when thinking about starting your own business, and most entrepreneurs need to seek funding for their first business venture. Finding out about where you might be able to secure investments will be important. Again, a mentor can help you with this.

- Consider working in a start-up company first to get some hands-on experience of what it is like to work in a small business that is still in its early days. This will give you vital insights into whether or not this is what you want in the longer term.

- Assess the risks and manage them. Setting up a business always involves taking a number of risks and a good mentor will help you to assess how great the particular risks are, and whether or not they are too great. They will also be able to help you to manage the risks as your plans progress.

○ If you decide that this is something you want to take forward, make a business plan.

Becoming an entrepreneur is something that many people consider and good entrepreneurs are vital to our economy. Most entrepreneurs would say that you need to be passionate about what you are doing, and prepared to work extremely hard. But they would also say that there is nothing like being your own boss and that the rewards can be great.

'By creating learning opportunities for myself...
I will be able to show my interest and passion as well as developing my competency.'

Case study : Digital profile

Tyrone is coming to the end of his summer job in a professional library and during his time there he has become much more aware of his digital profile and what it might say about him. He feels that if a prospective employer or recruiter looked at it, it would probably give a somewhat negative impression of him. Tyrone is keen to work on this over the summer before he goes back to university for the final year of his degree. He decides to open a new email account and to keep this solely for the purposes of applying for jobs and internships.

Having looked at his social media profile, he asks his group of close friends to remove particular pictures taken on nights out and he says he is happy to do the same for them if they want him to do so. He has taken a variety of pictures during his time at work and has also kept a journal. With the advice of his mentor, he decides to create a blog where he can store these and adds a link to this as part of his signature on his new email account. He also joins LinkedIn and starts to network with new people outside his circle to ask for tips and advice on how to get into publishing. He searches for himself regularly online, and over time is pleased that the first page of his results puts him across in a much more positive light.

Theme 11

Career decision making

This section will:

○ Introduce you to several different ways of making career decisions

○ Discuss rational decision making

○ Discuss the role of emotions in career decision making

○ Help you to consider the influence of limiting assumptions on your career development

○ Help you to think about making career decisions by focusing on the next steps in your development.

Decision making styles

People make career decisions in many different ways, and there is not a single or correct way of making a good career decision. Here are nine examples of different styles; they are listed in no particular order.

1 Impulsive – spontaneous and takes the first available option
2 Fatalistic – believes that fate will decide and so 'what will be, will be'
3 Compliant – heavily influenced by the views of other people and has a tendency to 'fall in line' with their wishes
4 Delayed – puts off making decisions constantly and consistently
5 Agonising – thinks everything through in minute detail
6 Planning – rational and balanced
7 Intuitive – focuses on their feelings
8 Escapist – avoids making decisions whenever possible
9 Play it safe – takes the route of least resistance.

Each of these decision making styles has its strengths and weaknesses, although some could be said to have more strengths than others. For example, other than a relaxed and stress-free life, it is difficult to think of strengths of the Escapist style; failure to make decisions tends to catch up with people sooner or later.

Many people make career decisions by using a combination of the styles listed above depending on the situation at the time. Equally, people can also make career decisions in different ways at different times depending on the circumstances they find themselves in. For example, someone who needs to find employment straight away might make a quick impulsive decision in order to pay their rent; at other times they might take a more measured approach. The well-known time management phrase 'procrastination is the thief of time' (see Theme 4.1) seems to apply well to career decision making, as putting off making a decision robs us of precious thinking time. Whilst we do not want to experience 'paralysis of analysis' by taking an overly Agonising approach, being forced into making a decision can easily lead to things we regret later on.

Try this   Looking at the styles from Theme 11.1, make a list of the strengths and weaknesses of each one. How have you made your career decisions in the past? For example, how did you choose your current course?

Rational decision making

Career decisions are often big decisions and many people would assume that a rational approach is best. In Theme 3.2 we discussed the importance of taking a strategic approach to your career development; if you are clear about what you want to do in the future, a rational or planned approach is a good one to take to help you to get there. In today's world, a career that only has one entry route is rare, so here are some steps you could follow if you know where you are heading.

1   How can you get to where you would like to be? Gather the information you need.
2   From this information, list the different routes into your chosen career area.
3   Write down the pros and cons of each route. Remember that an advantage for one person could be a disadvantage for someone else. It's your view that counts because you are the person who will be doing it.
4   Evaluate the routes and rank the options to establish what will work best for you. You could use a 'star' system to establish your preferences, with five stars being excellent and no stars being poor.
5   When you are happy with the ranking, decide the steps you need to take next.
6   Work on more than one option so you avoid 'putting all your eggs in one basket'.

Rational decision making can be a good approach but don't forget to think about the value of some of the other approaches too. For example, how do you feel about your options? The best option is not always the most logical one, particularly if you feel you won't enjoy it. It is always worth spending a bit of time re-evaluating what is important to you and looking back at where and how you might find career happiness (see Theme 3.3).

> 'I questioned whether or not I would be able to find a job in the career area I wished for, but also would I be qualified enough to achieve my dream career and get to where I wanted.'

The role of emotions in career decision making

For many years, people have argued that all good career decisions are planned and well thought-through; in other words, a rational career decision is always the best career decision. Often this involves a 'round peg in a round hole' approach where an individual examines themselves and the jobs available, and seeks as close a match as possible between the two. This may have been relevant in more predictable and stable economic times, but now it is widely recognised that there are many more factors that influence people's career decisions; one of these factors is the part that our emotions play in the decision making process.

It is now accepted that emotions have an important part to play in career decision making, and that being in tune with these helps us to make decisions more effectively. As discussed in Theme 11.2, taking a purely rational approach can mean that we do what we think is right logically, but we might then find ourselves doing something that we don't actually want to do – that is, if we get that far. Convincing an employer that we are interested in something when we aren't does not always work, as often it comes across in interviews. As a result, we might find ourselves facing lots of rejections.

Being in tune with our emotions involves a high level of EQ (as discussed in Theme 5.2) and, according to Emmerling and Cherniss (2003), we need the following four levels of skills in relation to our emotions.

1 Perceiving and expressing emotion – we need to know how we feel and be able to express this to others.
2 Assimilating emotion in thought – our emotions are integral to our thought processes and we can experience a range of emotions regarding the same thing at any one time. For example, we can feel excited about the future and scared at the same time. This level of skill involves weighing emotions against one another.
3 Understanding emotion – evaluating the range of emotions we experience helps us to understand our emotions better.

4 Managing emotions – when we have evaluated our emotions, we are in a better position to manage them.

Levels two to four each become more complex than the previous one and, if we can engage with all levels, we show that we have a high level of EQ overall.

We experience emotional reactions because of a range of factors. In relation to career decision making it is important to be aware of the influences other people can have on us from an emotional perspective. For example, wanting to please other people (such as parents and partners) can be a significant driving force, but we also need to remember that unless we are also doing what we want to do, career happiness (see Theme 3.3) can be elusive.

'At times I have let my emotions, fears and circumstances dictate my career journey rather than my passion.'

Try this   How do you feel about your future once you have graduated? Make a list of the emotions you are experiencing and the people who influence these.

Being aware of limiting assumptions

It is important to recognise that many of us have assumptions that can seriously restrict the way in which we view the future. If you have ever found yourself thinking or saying something along the lines of 'I could never do that because . . .', that might be correct, or, if you delve a little deeper, you could find that it is a limiting assumption. Many of us are too quick to discount ideas for the future, and very often it is easier to dismiss options rather than to research them. Challenging your limiting assumptions is an important element of career learning and development and is a vital step towards achieving your full potential.

Kline (1999) identifies the following three types of limiting assumption.

1   Facts – for example, 'I don't have the required qualifications'. It will always be important to check the detail here, as hearsay is not enough and cannot always be relied upon. In addition, it is worth remembering that things change rapidly, so what might have been the case in the past might not be so today. In addition, many careers have multiple routes of entry and some have conversion courses designed for people who do not have specified qualifications.
2   Possible facts – for example, 'my family or partner would not be supportive'. Again, until you check you cannot be sure; you might find that people are happier with your decisions than you expect.
3   Bedrock – for example, 'I won't be able to do that because I'm not good enough' or 'people like me don't do that'. These are assumptions we make about ourselves, how life works and where we fit in, and are deep-rooted. Often they act as barriers to career progression and can dilute our confidence and self-esteem. However, many of us are more capable than we think.

If you have found yourself dismissing things that interest you, and have rejected them because of some of the reasons shown in the examples above, it is probably worth revisiting them to see if you have made valid decisions. It is important to recognise that at times our assumptions are correct but sometimes they aren't. Limiting assumptions can be a way of avoiding challenges that we are capable of overcoming, and addressing them can be motivating and satisfying.

Try this

Think of times when you have thought or said 'I couldn't do that because ...' in relation to a career decision. Was this accurate? Or can you see evidence of Kline's three levels of assumptions?

Focusing on the next steps

As discussed in Theme 3.5 if the idea of career is still daunting, it often helps to think about your next steps rather than trying to look a long way ahead, as this lies within our ZPD (Vygotsky, 1978). As you get towards the end of your time in the workplace, you will undoubtedly have learned a lot about yourself and will have begun to consider what you might do following your graduation. Bearing in mind the constant and rapid changes in the labour market that are evident, looking for your next steps can be very helpful as it is flexible, and makes you more adaptable than someone who has a definite and fixed goal in mind. Identifying your next steps is usually easier than trying to decide what to do with the rest of your life – career decisions are rarely like this today anyway.

So what might your next steps be? Here are some possibilities.

○ Gaining employment – this is tricky if you are not clear about what you want to do. However, it can help you answer the ever-present question 'How do I know what I want to do until I do it'. But, of course, it will never be possible to try every job that exists, so reviewing Theme 3 should be helpful and give you some pointers.

○ Further placement or internship – this can be very helpful, particularly if you can gain a variety of experience in an organisation to enable you to explore a range of options.

○ Postgraduate study – this can give you some valuable extra thinking time and could 'set you apart' when making future job applications. However, there is such a thing as being overqualified; it is a mistake to assume that finding a job will always be easier with a higher degree.

○ Professional qualification – this is a good idea if you are clear about what you want to do. However, there is a danger in studying for one (such as a teaching or accountancy qualification) just as something to fall back on. You might find yourself with more debt (in the case of teaching) or lots of studying and examinations whilst working (in the case of accountancy) for something that you might not enjoy, and might never use in the future.

○ Time out – some people graduate and are ready for a break. Some decide to travel and this can be a good time to do so, as once you get settled into a job, taking an extended period of time off can be difficult. However, don't fall into the trap of thinking that during this time you will suddenly know what to do in the future. This rarely happens!

Thinking about your next steps can take some of the pressure off thinking about the future. Remember also that you will need to do this as you progress through your career journey. Few career decisions are made for life and we all need to review and revise them as we move forward to whatever we decide to do next.

For a long time, Amara has been unclear about what she wants to do in the future. She chose her degree in American Studies because she liked the sound of it in the prospectus. Lots of her friends were thinking about going to that particular university, so she decided she would go there too. Her parents were keen for her to go to 'a good university' so this decision kept them happy as well. In her spare time, she has been volunteering as a receptionist in a Citizens Advice Bureau and through this has seen people from many different walks of life facing a range of difficult situations. This experience is helping her to begin to think about what she wants to do after her graduation, and Amara decides to spend some time making some notes on the insights she is gaining that could help her in her decision making.

Through taking notes Amara realises that the most enjoyable part of volunteering is the contact she has with people. She enjoys the fact that no two days are the same, and she welcomes the opportunity to talk to people and to put them at ease. Many of the people she meets are coming for financial advice. Amara has never enjoyed maths and feels this is not one of her strengths, so she quickly rules out anything to do with finance and accountancy. Others come for legal advice and Amara enjoys talking to the legal advisers about the kind of support they can offer. She assumes that a career in the legal profession will not be possible because she is not studying for a degree in law. However, the advisers assure her that this is not the case, and on their advice she begins to look at law conversion courses. She also looks into other careers where she would be able to support people, and begins to consider social work and counselling.

Theme 12

Looking forward

This section will:

- ○ Help you to think about what you have gained from your time in the workplace
- ○ Enable you to consider what comes next in your personal and professional development
- ○ Help you to identify what you have to offer to an employer
- ○ Enable you to identify your next steps to help you to achieve your goals
- ○ Help you to be ready to make the most from your remaining time at university.

What have I gained from my time in the workplace?

We are now reaching the end of Part 1 and it is important to return to some key concepts that we have covered so far. In Theme 1.3 we looked at Kolb's (1984) experiential learning cycle and hopefully this journal has helped you to reflect on the many and varied experiences you have had in the workplace. Whether you have spent time on placement, been involved in an internship or volunteering, or have been working part-time to help with your finances, all of this will have given you important and useful experience on which to build.

Kolb's cycle encourages us to reflect on our experiences, so that we can apply the new knowledge we have gained to experiences in the future. So it is now important to look back and think about what you have learned over the past weeks and months. During your time in the workplace you will have had many different experiences and the Reflective Career Learning and Development Cycle in Figure 8 (based on the work of Kolb) will help you to think in more detail about what you have learned and how you might move forward. This cycle includes prompt questions to help you to think about your experience, including how you feel about it and any assumptions you might have been making.

It is important to understand that reflection and learning go 'hand in hand' and if we fail to reflect, we fail to learn, often because we simply forget.

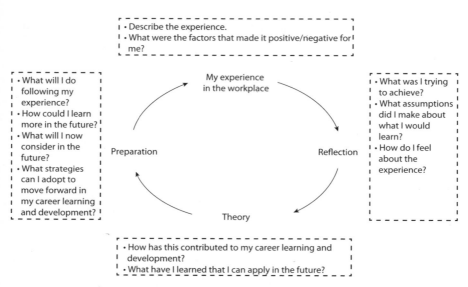

- Describe the experience.
- What were the factors that made it positive/negative for me?

- What will I do following my experience?
- How could I learn more in the future?
- What will I now consider in the future?
- What strategies can I adopt to move forward in my career learning and development?

My experience in the workplace

Preparation

Reflection

Theory

- What was I trying to achieve?
- What assumptions did I make about what I would learn?
- How do I feel about the experience?

- How has this contributed to my career learning and development?
- What have I learned that I can apply in the future?

Figure 8 The reflective career learning and development cycle

'I have taken positives from my learning experiences, especially in challenging situations as I can learn from them. I feel I am going from strength to strength.'

Try this

Look at each of the questions on the cycle in Figure 8 and write some responses to them.

What do I need to learn next?

In Theme 2.2 you undertook a SWOT/SWAIN analysis to examine particular aspects of your development, in order to become more self-aware. It would be good to go back to this now and to look at what you wrote. In particular, look at the following aspects as these will give you pointers to the things you need to learn next.

Weaknesses – which areas did you feel that you particularly needed to work on? How has this been going? What work do you still need to do?

Opportunities – which opportunities have you now taken advantage of and which have you missed? Make a list of the reasons why you did not take advantage of all the opportunities you had. What can you do to make sure you do not miss out on similar opportunities in the future?

Threats – what were the main threats to your development? Are they still present or have some of them now disappeared? Can you identify different threats now and, if so, what are they?

Aspirations – how have your aspirations changed? How would you describe your current aspirations?

Needs – understanding these is vital for your ongoing development. What are your current needs and your needs for the near future? Gaining your degree will be one of them, but what else? How do you now want to move forward in order to continue your career growth (see Theme 3.5)?

But as well as all of this, it is important to remember your strengths and interests. How have you continued to develop these? Have you been able to see new strengths and interests emerging, and, if so, what are they?

Taking some time to reflect on all of the above will be important for your development. It will also help you when it comes to making applications for jobs and further study, and in that all-important interview preparation. All employers want to talk to people who have thought about what they want to do and why they want to do it, and spending some time reflecting on what you have gained during your time in the workplace will aid your overall success.

Theme 12.3 What do I now have to offer?

As part of the SWOT/SWAIN analysis (see Theme 2.2) you were asked to think about your strengths and interests. It is vital not to forget these as interests help to keep us motivated; most of us are happy to do more of the things we enjoy. Strengths are important too as they build our confidence and resilience, and help us to feel satisfied and fulfilled; taking some time to think about them is very useful.

So, what would you now say are your key strengths? How have you continued to develop these? Where possible, having a specific response helps; so, for example, if IT is one of your particular strengths, which new programmes and devices have you now learned how to use? If you are a people person, which particular professional relationships have you now successfully built?

Undoubtedly your interests will also have developed over time. So what are your key interests currently? How have you developed these? In general, how do you make time for them? Are there times when you have allowed them to 'fall off the edge'?

It is well worth spending some time writing down what you now feel you have to offer to a potential employer. It could well be very different to what you might have written a few weeks or months ago, before you had the experience in the workplace that you now have. Again this will all provide useful general preparation for completing job applications and for updating your CV. You could also try writing down your top-five interests and strengths and ranking them, in order to gain a sharper focus.

Try this

Imagine you are writing a personal statement for a job you are really interested in. Write about what you now feel you have to offer the company or organisation.

What are my next steps?

In order to achieve career growth (see Theme 3.5) we need to be clear about our next steps. Looking ahead is not always easy, and you can identify your next steps in one of two ways. First, if you are now clear about what you want to do in the future, focus on this and work backwards. For example, if you know that you want a career in a particular type of accountancy, you can look at the professional qualifications you will need and the traineeships that might be on offer to help you to reach your goal. However, if you are still unclear about what you want to do (and many students are), it can be much more difficult. Some students hope that their time in the workplace will help them to become clearer about what the future holds, but then find their experience is not what they expected, and it only helps them to know what they no longer want to do; this can be confusing and unsettling. It might not feel like it, but at least being clear about what you don't want to do is a starting point. If you find yourself in this position, it is worth going back to Theme 8 and reviewing the things that you wrote; in particular, go back to your career anchors in Theme 8.1 and focus on what you really want from work. This should give you a starting point; following this, you could book a discussion with someone in your careers and employability department.

It is also worth remembering that you are probably entering another phase of transition. You might be returning to study at university, or your graduation might feel ever closer. Either way, understanding the transition process (see Theme 9.1) will be very helpful. In his seminal work on transitions, Bridges (2004) argues that all transitions have three stages; starting with 'endings', we experience loss as we begin to let go of what is soon to be behind us. It is worth remembering that even when we positively dislike our current situation, many of us prefer this to something new, because we do not like the unknown. 'Endings' are followed by what Bridges calls the 'neutral zone'; this is often an uncomfortable place where we feel anxious and uncertain about what lies ahead; here we can feel 'in limbo'. Bridges argues that we need to be sure to take some time here to discover what we should do next. If you feel confused and uncertain at the end of your time in the workplace, you may well be at this point in the transition process. The 'neutral zone' is followed by 'new beginnings', as we move forward into the next phase of our lives. It is worth noting that the three stages overlap; this means that we can still be experiencing loss, whilst feeling uncertain about the future even after we have begun something new.

Career growth, like any other kind of growth, is likely to be a lengthy but vital process. We all know what happens to plants that grow very quickly; usually their roots are shallow, and many of them turn out to be weeds! If you find yourself in a rush to grow, it is fine to slow down and to take some time, so long as your finances allow this of course. This could mean getting more experience, taking time out to volunteer or to travel, or continuing your studies at postgraduate level.

'I will always feel a sense of loss even when I am excited about a new beginning.'

Try this   Think about Bridges' transition model. Where are you in the three-stage process?

Back to university and back to study

Spending some time in the workplace on placement or doing an internship can be extremely helpful in many ways, but when it comes to an end, it will then be time to return to your studies. Settling back into student life is not always as easy as it sounds, particularly if you have had a whole academic year out. Undoubtedly some of your friends will have graduated already and, if your year out was optional, you will be studying alongside new people from the year below. There may also be new members of staff to get to know.

Academic years are notoriously short, so it will be important to get back into the swing of things quickly so you do not lose valuable time. Things like accommodation and finance will need some forward planning. Be sure to register for your final year in time and check that your IT and library accounts are current. You may also be asked about supervision if your final year includes a dissertation, and you could think about undertaking a project with your employer as your dissertation topic, in order to maintain your valuable contacts. If possible, choose optional modules that fit in with the experience you have had on placement. That way you will maximise your learning from the workplace.

On a more general level it is good to think about all the useful habits that you have picked up whilst at work, for example getting up early and organising your time well. These are well worth continuing once you are back at university as they will give you well-earned free time at weekends.

Once the academic year gets started (or even before) you will want to start looking for your next step after graduation. Many popular graduate schemes and postgraduate courses start their recruitment very early, so be sure not to miss out by leaving things too late. Don't forget to look forward to that graduation ceremony either and when it comes, be sure to celebrate your achievement – you will have earned it!

Case study: Career confusion

Sarah is studying for a degree in economics and for a while has been interested in banking. She took a year out to do a placement in a corporate investment bank in their mergers and acquisitions department. She enjoyed it to begin with, but after a while she began to find that there were some aspects of the work that she disliked. She found the atmosphere rather formal, highly stressful and extremely target-driven. The working hours were very long and the expectation was that people would stay until work was completed. She began to find herself working at the weekends, often going into the office on Saturdays and some Sundays.

In spite of all of this, Sarah decided to complete her placement as she felt she was gaining useful experience and enhancing her CV. Even before the end of her placement she knew that she no longer wanted to work in a bank when she graduated, and went through a period of time feeling she had no idea what she wanted to do. However, gradually, she was able to identify the aspects of the work that she had enjoyed, especially during the early days of the placement. She was also able to understand what she had really hoped for before she started (for example, contact with people and offering some kind of service) and began to look at other careers related to finance that would give her more career happiness and a better work–life balance. In particular, she began to look at financial opportunities in the public sector and decided to apply for short-term internships to explore this further following graduation.

Part 2

More space for reflection

Part 2 gives you more space for reflective writing and contains a number of activities as more 'food for thought'. The activities are designed to help you to reflect on the variety of experiences you have been having in the workplace. They encourage you to look back and to look forward to the future. You will be able to use much of what you write as you prepare for what you will do following your graduation – such as applying for jobs and courses, and preparing for interviews. How you use these pages is up to you and you should feel free to complete the various activities when it makes most sense for you to do so. Remember to date your writing, as in the future it will probably be difficult to remember this kind of detail and it is useful to track your development over time.

My first day

Write a description of how you felt on your first day in the workplace. How do you feel now and how has your thinking changed?

Try this   *'Light-bulb' moments*

During your time on placement it is quite likely that you will have experienced some 'light-bulb moments'. These can be described as instances when things that you have struggled with suddenly begin to make sense. Use this space to keep a note of them as they happen. Later on they could provide you with excellent examples of things to discuss at interview.

Try this   *The most interesting and fulfilling part of your time in the workplace*

Looking back, what have been the most interesting aspects of your time in the workplace? Take some time to think about why this was. Now think about the most fulfilling parts. In particular, what did you find fulfilling and why? How does all of this relate to your 'career anchors'? (See Theme 8.1.) This kind of self-knowledge can help you in your career decision making in the future.

'I realise I am most motivated when interested and satisfied with the challenge.'

Try this *The most challenging part of your time in the workplace*

During your placement you will have come across many challenges. Use this space to document them and think about what was challenging about them. These can give you important pointers to things that you need to work on in your professional development. Remember they could relate to skills (for example, IT, communication, teamwork), knowledge (for example, of appropriate legislation, policies, procedures) and attitudes (for example, motivation, confidence, commitment).

'Today my placement was really hard and left me feeling physically and mentally drained.'

My old CV

Having a strong CV will be vital when it comes to searching for a job. Most people have a CV and it is important that you keep it up to date, so that if something that you are interested in applying for comes up, you are in a good position to apply for it quickly. Even when jobs have a closing date, it is important to remember that some employers stop taking applications as soon as they consider they have received enough in order to see a good pool of people. Spend some time critically evaluating your CV. What is good about it? Where can it be improved and updated? Now think about when you will do this and who you could show it to for some feedback.

'Generally, I just go for the first job I see. I'm never sure if this is fate telling me to do something or just my boredom kicking in again!'

Try this   *The 'wisdom of hindsight'*

Looking back and reflecting on our experiences is something that we can gain a lot from. Often we can look back and wish that we had done things differently. If you had your time in the workplace again, what would you do differently? What would you do more of? What would you do less of? Which particular opportunities would you choose to focus on? This kind of activity can give you useful insights into your future career development.

Try this

Networking

Make a list of the key people you have networked with. How will you keep in touch with them? Remember that building contacts can be a vital way of accessing the informal job market (see Theme 10.1).

Try this

My 'standout' moment

When you look back on your time in the workplace, what single thing will you always remember? If you can't narrow it down to one thing, try thinking of three things and then ranking them. These will provide excellent examples that you can talk about at interview.

Try this   *The letter to my manager I will never send*

Most people have difficult times on placement as well as good times. Think about a time when you faced difficulties; it might even be that there were times when you thought about leaving. What would you have liked to be able to say to your manager at that time? Write a letter to put this into words. How would you address those challenges now? Many employers ask about challenges and how you have addressed them when interviewing candidates.

Try this

My placement journey

Draw a picture or diagram of your time in the workplace. Remember that you do not need to be artistic to do this; it can be as simple as a graph with peaks and troughs.

Try this

What does my future look like now?

Looking at your drawing or diagram, now think about the way ahead and try to depict it in another picture or diagram.

'I was told not to assume I would get the job just because I have experience working for the company.'

Try this   *My goals*

Look back at your goals from Theme 1.2. How far have you achieved them? In which areas have you made most progress and why? Where have you not made as much progress as you wanted, and why not? What might you need to do next? Remember we can sometimes set goals that at the time we think are realistic, but turn out not to be so later on. This is not about 'beating yourself up' about things you haven't been able to achieve, particularly if they are outside your control. Sometimes though we can gain insights into areas where we need to be more focused in order to succeed.

Try this   *Where am I now on my career journey?*

Think about where you have reached on your career journey. This could include being clearer about your next steps, but equally it could be that you recognise a need to rethink your plans. You could even be more confused than when your placement started. If so, who will you go to for support?

'I wish I had someone who could just tell me what to do; I hate the not knowing.'

Try this

Where do I want to be by the time I graduate?

Imagine it is the day of your graduation ceremony; where do you hope to be in relation to your career development?

Try this

Five years from now

Imagine it is now five years since you graduated. Where do you want to be and what do you hope you will be doing? Be sure to think generally as well as specifically.

My values

Make a list of the key words that express your personal values in relation to work. Which ones do you feel are the most important?

Try this

What is important to me and makes me happy?

If you inherited a large amount of money and no longer needed to work, how would you choose to spend your time?

Try this

My achievements

Make a list of your key achievements. These could be academic, personal and work-based. These will provide good material for personal statements and letters of application for jobs.

Try this   *My career decisions*

Spend some time thinking about how you got to where you are now. Here are some questions that can help to guide you.

Where am I now?
How did I get here?
How did I make my decisions?

Rank your decisions using the following scale.

5 = Excellent
4 = Good
3 = OK
2 = Not good
1 = Not good at all

What does this show you about how you have made your decisions and how you might make them in the future?

More space for reflection

Try this

The perspectives of others

Imagine you overhear two colleagues talking about you in relation to your professional work. What do you hope they will be saying?

Part 3
CV Building

Having a well-developed and up-to-date CV is vital when you get to the point where you want to start looking for work. Whether this is following graduation or during your degree, having a CV that encapsulates what you have done will be important. However, many people need to tailor their CV for particular applications, so over a period of time you are likely to find that you have more than one version. Building your CV takes time and after a while it is easy to forget things that you have done, even those things that at the time really stood out to you. Part 3 is designed to give you a tool for doing this and is a record that you will be able to return to as the need arises. Taking a bit of time to record what you have done whilst in the workplace will undoubtedly save you precious time in the future.

Log for work/placement experience

Make a list of the different periods of time you have spent in the workplace with dates and key contacts. Use the column on the right to describe briefly the experience you gained.

Dates	Organisation	Key contacts	Experience gained

Training courses attended

Use the grid below to make a list of the training courses you have attended and what you gained from them.

Dates	Course	Place	Documents/Certificates

Meetings attended

During your time in the workplace you will probably attend lots of meetings. Use the table below to make a list of them; put regular meetings, such as team meetings, together in a group.

Dates	Meeting	Role in the meeting	Actions and activities

Projects completed

Use the space below to write a short description of projects you have been involved in and the things you feel you have achieved through your involvement.

Dates	Name of project	Role played in the project	Key achievements

Core skills

Describe your core skills under the following headings. Use the right-hand column to make a note of things that you need to work on.

Core skills	Development points
Communication – Oral With individuals With groups In meetings Other	
Communication – Written Reports Minutes of meetings Client notes Formal letters Other	

Communication – ICT Emails Word processing Spreadsheets Presentations Other	
Numeracy Budgets Expenses Statistics Other	
Teamwork – your role in a team Leadership skills Problem solving Analytical skills Organisational skills Creativity Resilience	

Key contacts

Use the table below to keep a record of key people you have come into contact with.

Dates	Name	Place/Organisation	Notes

Presentations given

Use this space to record any presentations you have made and use the column on the right to write notes on any feedback you received.

Dates	Title of presentation	Context	Feedback received

Applications made

Use the table below to keep a record of applications you have made.

Dates	Job/role	Organisation	Notes

References

Adams, J., Hayes, J. and Hopson, B. (1976) *Transition: Understanding and Managing Personal Change,* London: Martin Robertson.

Barnes, A., Bassot, B. and Chant, A. (2011) *A Practical Guide to Career Learning and Development: Innovation in Careers Education 11–19,* Abingdon: Routledge.

Bassot, B. (2009) 'Career Learning and Development: A Bridge to the Future', in H.L. Reid (ed.), *Constructing the Future: Career Guidance for Changing Contexts,* Stourbridge: Institute of Career Guidance.

Bassot, B., Barnes, A. and Chant, A. (2014) *A Practical Guide to Career Learning and Development: Innovation in Career Education 11–19,* Abingdon: Routledge.

Belbin, R. M. (1993) *Team Roles at Work,* Oxford: Butterworth-Heinemann.

Bridges, W. (2004) *Transitions, Making Sense of Life's Changes,* Boston, MA: Da Capo Press.

Covey, S. (2004a) *The 7 Habits of Highly Effective People: Restoring the Character Ethic,* New York: Free Press.

Covey, S. R. (2004b) *The 8th Habit: From Effectiveness to Greatness,* New York: Free Press.

Csíkszentmihályi, M. (1990) *Flow: The Psychology of Optimal Experience,* New York: Harper and Row.

Dacre Pool, L. and Sewell, P. (2007) 'The Key to Employability: Developing a Practical Model of Graduate Employability', *Education & Training,* Vol. 49, No. 4, pp. 277–89.

Driffield, N. L., Foster, C. S. and Higson, H. E. (2011) 'Placements and Degree Performance: Do Placements Lead to Better Marks, Or Do Better Students Choose Placements?' in D. Siva-Jothy (ed.), *ASET Annual Conference 2011: Research Papers from Placement and Employability Professionals' Conference 2011.* ASET, Sheffield (UK), pp. 4–27, ASET Annual Conference, Leeds, United Kingdom, 6–8 September.

Edwards, R. (1993) 'The Inevitable Future? Post-Fordism in Work and Learning' in R. Edwards, S. Sieminski and D. Zeldin (eds), *Adult Learners, Education and Training,* London: Routledge, pp.176–86.

Emmerling, R. J. and Cherniss, C. (2003) 'Emotional Intelligence and the Career Choice Process', *Journal of Career Assessment,* Vol. 11, No. 2, pp. 153–67.

Eraut, M. (2006) 'Editorial', *Learning in Health and Social Care,* Vol. 5, No. 3, pp. 111–18.

Fontana, D. (2005) *Managing Stress,* London: BPS Books with Routledge.

Goleman, D. (1996) *Emotional Intelligence: Why It Can Matter More Than IQ,* London: Bloomsbury Publishing.

Handy, C. (1993) *Understanding Organizations,* Oxford: Oxford University Press.

Hicks, T. (2016) 'Seven Steps for Effective Problem Solving in the Workplace', Mediate, www.mediate.com/articles/thicks.cfm, date accessed 9 July 2016.

Honey, P. and Mumford, A. (2000) *The Learning Styles Helper's Guide,* Maidenhead: Peter Honey Publications.

Honey, P. and Mumford, A. (2006) *The Learning Styles Questionnaire,* (revised edition), Maidenhead: Peter Honey Publications Ltd.

Keyes, C., Shmotkin, D. and Ryff, C. (2002) 'Optimizing Well-Being: The Empirical Encounter of Two Traditions', *Journal of Personality and Social Psychology,* Vol. 82, No. 6, 1007–22.

Kline, N. (1999) *Time to Think,* London: Ward Lock.

Kolb, D. (1984) *Experiential Learning: Experience as the Source of Learning and Development,* New Jersey: Prentice Hall.

Lindenfield, G. (2014) *Assert Yourself: Simple Steps to Build your Confidence,* London: HarperThorsons.

Luft, H. (1984) *Group Processes: An Introduction to Group Dynamics*, Mountain View, CA: Mayfield.

Noon, M. and Blyton, P. (2007) *The Realities of Work*, Basingstoke: Palgrave Macmillan.

Schein, E. H. and Van Maanen, J. (2013) *Career Anchors*, 4th edn, San Francisco, CA: Wiley.

Storey, J. A. (2000) '"Fracture Lines" in the Career Environment' in A. Collin and R. A. Young (eds), *The Future of Career*, Cambridge: Cambridge University Press, pp.21–36.

Vygotsky, L. S. (1978) *Mind in Society*, Cambridge, MA: Harvard University Press.

Yorke, M. (2006) '*Employability in Higher Education: What It Is – What It Is Not*', York: The Higher Education Academy.

Index